Women's Work and Public Policy

Kathleen A. Laughlin

Women's Work and Public Policy

A HISTORY OF
THE WOMEN'S BUREAU,
U.S. DEPARTMENT OF LABOR
1945–1970

NORTHEASTERN UNIVERSITY PRESS
Boston

Northeastern University Press 2000

Library of Congress Cataloging-in-Publication Data
Laughlin, Kathleen A.
Women's work and public policy : a history of the Women's Bureau, U.S.
Department of Labor, 1945-1970 / Kathleen A. Laughlin.
p. cm.
Based on the author's dissertation presented to Ohio State University.
Includes bibliographical references and index.
ISBN 1-55553-444-9
1. United States. Women's Bureau—History. 2. Women—Employment—
Government policy—United States—History. I. Title.

HD6095 .L35 2000
945'.77—dc21   99-058664

Portions of Chapter 4 appeared in "Sisterhood Inc.: The Status of
Women Commission Movement and the Rise of Feminist Coalition
in Ohio, 1964-1974," *Ohio History* 108 (Winter-Spring 1999).
Courtesy of the Ohio Historical Society.

Designed by inari

Composed in Sabon by inari in Bloomington, Indiana.
Printed and bound by The Maple Press Company in York, Pennsylvania.
The paper is Sebago Antique Cream, an acid-free sheet.

MANUFACTURED IN THE UNITED STATES OF AMERICA
04 03 02 01 00   5 4 3 2 1

for Willa

Contents

Acknowledgments

THIS BOOK BEGAN several years ago as a dissertation at The Ohio State University. Leila Rupp's and Warren Van Tine's insightful criticism during the dissertation process charted the direction of my subsequent revisions. I thank them for their support during my graduate school years. The following funding sources from Ohio State University subsidized research in the Women's Bureau's records at the National Archives: the Ruth Higgins Fellowship, Department of History, Elizabeth Gee Grant, Center for Women's Studies, and the Alumni Research Grant. An Arthur and Elizabeth Schlesinger Library Dissertation Grant and a grant from the John F. Kennedy Library also supported the project in its initial stages.

The transformation of an institutional history of the Women's Bureau to a broader study considering the activities of several women's organizations would not have been possible without additional support from many quarters. Cynthia Harrison's critical comments on my book proposal improved my arguments. Metropolitan State University professional improvement grants funded research trips to organizational archives and the Library of Congress. Archivists Susan McGrath, National Archives for Black Women's History, and Dorothy Wick and Elizabeth Norris at the YWCA's National Office gave unsparingly of their time and cheerfully shared their expertise with me. I am also grateful to archivists at the National Archives and the Library of Congress. I wish to thank former and current Women's Bureau staff members for sharing information about their working lives: Trinice Clayborne, Diane Crothers, Mary Hilton, Roberta McKay, Ruth Nadel, Ruth Shinn, Isabel Streidel, and Jane Walstedt. A position as a visiting scholar at the Institute for Research on Women, Douglass College, Rutgers University, gave me the time and support to begin to prepare the manuscript for publication. I am especially grateful to Beth Hutchinson for her assistance during my residency at Rutgers.

I am indebted to colleagues at Metropolitan State University who eased my burden as program coordinator of the Women's Studies Program so that I could maintain a commitment to research and writing. Many thanks to Daniel Abebe, Anne Aronson, Nancy Black, Mary Brekke, Susan Giguere, Bob Gremore, Karen Gulliver, Carol Holmberg, Maythee Kantor, Nantawan Lewis, Carol Lowe, Chet Meyers, Miriam Meyers, Anne Phibbs, Jacqueline Richardson, Doug Rossinow, Anne Webb, Carolyn Whitson, flo wiger, and Dean of the College of Arts and Sciences Fred Kirchhoff.

I wish to thank several people at Northeastern University Press for helping me to prepare this manuscript for publication: Jill Bahcall, Emily McKeigue, John Weingartner, and Jennifer Wilkin. I am particularly grateful to Terri Teleen for her enthusiastic support of my project.

My parents, Joanne and James Laughlin, and my sister, Suzanne Laughlin, provided pleasant diversions when I needed them most.

I am most indebted to Willa Young and Susan M. Hartmann, who read enough versions of this manuscript to qualify as honorary Washington bureaucrats. Susan Hartmann remained interested in this project and in my career long after her duty as dissertation director was at an end. Her critical comments during the manuscript's many stages strengthened my arguments and prose, but I am most grateful for her encouragement and kind attention when my commitment and confidence wavered. She exemplifies the kind of women's historian I hope to become, an excellent teacher, a productive scholar, and an attentive mentor. Willa Young's friendship and love sustained me throughout this project. Her commitment to social change as a contemporary professional activist continues to inspire me. This book is dedicated to her.

Abbreviations

AAUW American Association of University Women
AFL American Federation of Labor
BLS Bureau of Labor Statistics
BFOQ Bona Fide Occupational Qualification
BPW National Federation of Business and Professional Women's
  Clubs
CACSW Citizens' Advisory Council on the Status of Women
CIO Congress of Industrial Organizations
EEOC Equal Employment Opportunity Commission
EOF Earning Opportunities Forum for Mature Women
ERA Equal Rights Amendment
FLSA Fair Labor Standards Act
ICSW Interdepartmental Committee on the Status of Women
LWV League of Women Voters
NCCW National Council of Catholic Women
NCEP National Committee for Equal Pay
NCJW National Council of Jewish Women
NCL National Consumers' League
NCNW National Council of Negro Women
NOW National Organization for Women
NWCCR National Women's Committee for Civil Rights
NWP National Woman's Party
OMAT Office of Manpower, Automation, and Training
OMER Office of Manpower Evaluation and Research
PCSW President's Commission on the Status of Women
UAW United Automobile, Aircraft, and Agricultural Workers of
  America
UE United Electrical Workers
USES United States Employment Service
WHPC Wage, Hour, and Public Contracts Divisions
WICS Women in Community Service
YWCA Young Women's Christian Association

Women's Work and Public Policy

Introduction

*Never doubt that a small group of thoughtful, committed
citizens can change the world; indeed, it's the only thing
that ever does.*

—Margaret Mead

KAREN NUSSBAUM, appointed by President Bill Clinton to serve as
the thirteenth director of the Women's Bureau, hosted the agency's
seventy-fifth anniversary celebration in 1995. Diana Jenkins and
her friends from the Ohio State University chapter of 9 to 5, the
National Association for Working Women, that Nussbaum had
founded in 1977, came to Washington, D.C., for the anniversary
conference. During the two-day meeting, the Columbus, Ohio,
group met with veteran women's rights activists, including retired
career bureaucrats from the Women's Bureau who were honored at
the conference for service to the nation's working women. Jenkins
and her colleagues were surprised to learn that feminists had toiled
in the federal government during the 1940s, 1950s, and 1960s.[1]
They had no idea that the small agency in the Labor Department
has, since its inception in 1920, tried to change the world by forming alliances with policy partners—women's organizations, state
and federal agencies, businesses, and unions throughout the country. When Diana Jenkins returned to Ohio with information about
women's rights under the Pregnancy Discrimination Act, the Civil
Rights Act, and the Family and Medical Leave Act to share with
her constituents, she repeated the experience of a long line of individuals who connected the Women's Bureau to its grassroots constituency.

Policy partners such as Jenkins helped the Women's Bureau
circulate a national questionnaire in 1993 asking wage-earning
women to relate their attitudes toward full-time employment and to
describe their experiences in the workplace. The ambitious survey
of women's lives represented Clinton's initiative to "reinvent gov-

ernment" by making federal agencies more responsive to the public. The questionnaire, "linking government and the grassroots," generated over a quarter of a million replies.[2] By revealing that "79% of survey respondents 'like' or 'love' their jobs overall" and that "women take pride and satisfaction at being breadwinners for their families and a significant part of the American workplace," the results contradicted contemporary images of harried women trying to succeed at home and at work and not doing either very well.[3] The survey continued a long tradition in the Women's Bureau of using research, publicity, and cooperation with allies in the private sector to challenge the persistent stereotype that women do not share men's commitment or need to work. This confluence of tactics and ideology characterizes the bureau's seventy-five-year history.

This book explains how the Women's Bureau's practice of "linking government and the grassroots" helped to sustain the political milieu for women's rights activism during the post–World War II era and for resurgent feminism in the 1960s. The bureau's strategic use of resources, such as national conferences, a system of regional field representatives, and a research and public relations staff, enabled it to encourage programmatic continuity and political activism among labor union women and disparate religious, civic, service, and professional women's organizations after World War II. This coalition, in addition to trade unionists, included the National Council of Catholic Women (NCCW), the League of Women Voters (LWV), the American Association of University Women (AAUW), the National Council of Negro Women (NCNW), the National Federation of Business and Professional Women's Clubs (BPW), the National Council of Jewish Women (NCJW), and the Young Women's Christian Association (YWCA). By the mid-1960s, the Women's Bureau, as the administrative catalyst behind equal rights campaigns led by spin-offs from President John F. Kennedy's Commission on the Status of Women—the Citizens' Advisory Council on the Status of Women and state commissions on the status of women—drew the postwar coalition into social movements for state and federal policies on women's issues. In examining how policy formation within the federal government facilitated the development of women's rights networks across race, class, and ideological lines, this study, like the research of Nancy Gabin and Dorothy Sue Cobble on feminist activism in labor unions and organizational histories of the AAUW, the YWCA, and the National Woman's Party, documents continuity between postwar activism and social movement feminism in the 1960s.[4]

Several scholars have recognized the Women's Bureau's role in achieving two policy victories in the 1960s: the formation of the President's Commission on the Status of Women (PCSW) in 1961 and passage of the Equal Pay Act of 1963, which evoked a national commitment to achieving equal employment opportunities for women.[5] Why and how did the Women's Bureau succeed in furthering an equal rights program in the 1960s even though it advocated state protective labor legislation for women—laws regulating daily hours, night work and weight lifting, and stipulating requirements for seating, rest areas, lunch periods, and a minimum wage—predicated on an ideology that family responsibilities made women less equipped than men to meet the demands of work? Standard explanations give Esther Peterson, President Kennedy's closest female adviser and the Women's Bureau's fourth director, most of the credit for orchestrating women's rights policies within the federal government as a means to undermine support for the Equal Rights Amendment. Peterson, as two other Bureau directors before her, Mary Anderson and Frieda Miller, feared that an equal rights amendment to the Constitution would invalidate existing protective labor laws aimed at regulating the workplace for women. The Women's Bureau's inability to achieve concrete federal responses to women's issues, until Peterson orchestrated her political coup against ERA proponents, has stigmatized it as ineffective in shaping policies but important enough to drive a wedge in the women's movement over protective labor legislation versus the ERA as the best way to ameliorate women's economic status.[6]

I revise the standard interpretation by suggesting that protective labor laws actually facilitated continuity between policymaking in the Women's Bureau during the postwar years and the rise of the modern feminist movement in the 1960s. The Women's Bureau's advocacy of state labor laws to raise women's wages indicates more progressive intentions than historians have assumed. Most notably, the historian Alice Kessler-Harris has suggested that the Women's Bureau updated justifications for protective labor laws to be consistent with the exigencies of a postwar consumer economy dependent on women's work without modifying policy goals that considered women's individual rights or challenged the persistence of a sex-segregated labor market.[7] What is missing in this analysis is the Women's Bureau's role in establishing an active network of allies in the private sector to promote women's employment rights consistent with ideological readjustments. Postwar policy formation in the bureau favored an exclusive focus on laws to increase women's wages and a commitment to the placement of women as a permanent part of the labor force in response to national economic policies, the ideologies of presidential administrations, and the changing status of constituency groups. Consequently, after 1945, active advancement of protective labor legislation based on assumptions of women's physical and emotional inferiority to male workers, such as restrictions on night work and regulations dictating working conditions, suffered from benign neglect. At the same time, state minimum wage, maximum hours, and equal pay laws offered the Women's Bureau policymaking footholds in state governments and the potential for expansion of staff and functions that an equal rights amendment would not have provided.

Even though bureaucratic constraints prevented the bureau from publicly deviating from its statutory mission of supporting both restrictive laws and laws aimed at increasing women's wages, its permanent, albeit small (less than one hundred), staff of economists, career counselors, attorneys, and public relations experts incubated and sustained a postwar women's economic agenda: legislation to equalize wage rates between men and women, career and job placement initiatives, and a federal commission to study the status of women. Labor union women, organizations, and state and local governments depended on the only federal agency representing women until the 1960s for research on women's economic contributions, legal expertise in drafting legislation, and public relations connections, including the ability to host national conferences on women's issues. My analysis that the Women's Bureau's backstage activism differed from center stage advocacy of restrictive protective labor laws is consistent with an interpretation of policy formation called the "state-centered approach," which suggests that the state originates and promotes political goals through the control of resources.[8] The conceptual framework of center stage and backstage behavior explains the paradoxical

nature of the Women's Bureau's history as the institutional location of both maternalist and equal rights policies.

By applying a gender analysis to policy formation from the
Progressive Era until World War II, numerous scholars have traced
the source of women's inequality in the welfare state to "maternal-
ists"—middle-class reformers and professionals responsible for shaping social welfare policy related to women's maternal role from the
Progressive Era to Franklin Roosevelt's New Deal in the 1930s.[9]
Protective labor legislation was a maternalist public policy. In a
political and judicial climate that championed the individual's right
to contract freely with employers, social welfare reformers active in
the National Women's Trade Union League and the National Consumers' League defended the constitutionality of state protective
labor laws for women on the principle that female workers, as
mothers to future citizens, should be wards of the state. The Supreme
Court accepted this female difference argument in upholding the
constitutionality of the State of Oregon's maximum hours law for
women in *Muller v. Oregon* (1908).

The Women's Bureau, a product of Progressive Era social welfare and suffrage activism, became one of the bureaucratic execu-
tors of maternalist public policies, as is clear from its statutory
mission "to formulate standards and policies which shall promote
the welfare of wage-earning women, improve their working conditions, increase their efficiency, and advance their opportunities for
profitable employment."[10] Robyn Muncy's study on the "reform
culture" that gave rise to the welfare state indicates that the Children's Bureau and Women's Bureau in the Labor Department kept
the reform impulse of the Progressive Era alive during the 1920s
and 1930s.[11] Mary Anderson, director of the Women's Bureau from
1920 to 1944, supervised on-site factory investigations to record
working conditions that threatened women's health. This research
orientation established a factual basis for state protective labor
laws advocated by women's organizations, with the notable exception of the National Woman's Party, a proponent of the Equal
Rights Amendment, which threatened sex-based legislation. According to historians, the long-standing rivalry over protective labor legislation in the post-suffrage years stalled organized campaigns for
women's rights until the 1960s.[12]

Even though restrictive protective labor legislation occupied the Women's Bureau in the 1920s and 1930s, Mary Anderson and her staff resisted blanket discriminatory legislation and public prejudices that denied women the right to enter the labor market or justified unequal pay scales. Historians have affirmed the Women's Bureau's efforts to insert equal pay clauses in the National Recovery Act codes during the Great Depression.[13] Moreover, when the economic crisis led to the passage of "married women bills" in twenty-four state legislatures to place men in publicly funded jobs traditionally held by women, such as teaching, public health, social work, and positions in libraries, the presence of legal discrimination shifted the bureau's investigatory focus from working conditions studies to documentation of the importance of women's income to families.[14] The shift in research focus indicates the precarious hold of the difference argument over actual activities. Thus, the split between ideological imperatives and policy formation occurred even then.

Even after the Fair Labor Standards Act of 1938 (FLSA) cleared the way for codifying protective labor standards for men, the Women's Bureau maintained an ideology of women's essential difference from men and stood by state labor laws for women as a separate class of workers. Judith Sealander attributed this attachment to the past to the work of career bureaucrats schooled in Progressive Era reform who remained at the bureau until the 1950s. She called them "outsiders as insiders": "As 'outsiders,' they frequently encountered condescension and indifference from their own administrative superiors. As 'insiders,' they were hostage to the traditional view of ideal women as helpmates and homemakers."[15] Patricia Zelman's explanation of the prominence of protective labor laws in the bureau's policy repertoire during this period emphasized the fact that existing state labor laws governing women's employment set better standards than could be achieved with the FLSA.[16]

"Insider" and "outsider" status changed the Women's Bureau's policies after World War II in ways that Sealander underemphasizes. As an "insider" the bureau had to respond to the manpower and economic planning mission within the Labor Department, dictated by the 1946 Employment Act, focused on maintaining high levels of employment and easing shortages in skilled occupations. During

Dwight D. Eisenhower's administration in particular, employment placement programs dominated Labor Department activities within an administration that downplayed the federal government's regulatory role in order to facilitate a partnership with business. The bureau's "outsider" status that demanded an alliance with women's organizations required similar policy adjustments. Gwendolyn Mink ends her study on maternalist policies and the formation of the welfare state before World War II because "that war opened a new era for women. White married women entered the wage labor force in unprecedented numbers, many to stay. A new generation of political women came of age, many of whom subordinated the politics of motherhood to a new politics of opportunity."[17] The "new politics of opportunity" aptly describes the orientation of prominent postwar policy partners, especially the Business and Professional Women's Clubs, the American Association of University Women, and labor union women.

As a federal agency without enforcement authority and dependent on public approval, the Women's Bureau disguised political activities and shifting priorities by creating additional committees and programs consistent with the "new politics of opportunity" that functioned in public as auxiliary citizens' groups of women's organizations and unions. In the 1940s, its Labor Advisory Committee sustained networks among union women in order to promote federal and state equal pay legislation. A decade later during the Eisenhower administration, the BPW took over a career and job placement program under Women's Bureau sponsorship called Earning Opportunities Forum. The National Women's Committee for Civil Rights (NWCCR), organized by the bureau's staff to enlist black and white women's organizations in a campaign to advance President John F. Kennedy's civil rights agenda in the South, became a private group with an executive director. Another interracial coalition coordinated by the Women's Bureau, the Women in Community Service (WICS), made sure Lyndon B. Johnson's War on Poverty programs considered the needs of women and girls. These auxiliary advisory panels, not constrained by the need for "bureaucratic neutrality," represented Bureau attempts to generate grassroots movements for employment rights.[18]

Status of women's groups created by the President's Commission on the Status of Women—the Citizens' Advisory Council on the

Status of Women, the Interdepartmental Committee on the Status of Women, and state governors' commissions on the status of women— maintained the tradition of stealth policymaking, because, as Georgia Duerst-Lahti argues, they were free to develop independent agendas and critique insider politics.[19] At times upstart commissions and advisory committees embraced the Equal Rights Amendment and denounced the discriminatory aspects of protective labor laws, which put the Women's Bureau in the awkward position of providing resources to groups that rejected its traditional mission. But the bureau's staff soon recognized that status of women institutions provided more powerful rationales for the maintenance of a separate women's agency than the anachronistic women's difference argument afforded by consistent advocacy of protective labor legislation. New organizational mandates to monitor progress toward equity within federal programs, to develop additional policies in accordance with the PCSW's recommendations, and to stimulate state commission movements put the Women's Bureau in the business of publicly sanctioned feminist organizing by the mid-1960s.

This history of the Women's Bureau's policies after World War II proves Margaret Mead's statement that "a small group of thoughtful, committed citizens can change the world." The Women's Bureau's backstage maneuvering around established bureaucratic constraints to promote the women's economic agenda in the postwar years led to center stage feminist advocacy within and outside of the federal government by the 1970s. The first two chapters, which consider the 1940s and 1950s, place the Women's Bureau in the political world of cycles of bureaucratic retrenchment, stingy congressional appropriations, and indifferent labor secretaries, all of which prevented any public deviation from its statutory mission. Facing significant budget cuts, labor secretaries in the Truman and Eisenhower administrations sought to streamline functions, which included several attempts to wipe out the constituency-based women's agency. If women had the same needs and interests as men, a separate agency to represent them would not be necessary. However, organizational changes within the Labor Department required the Women's Bureau to share the full employment mission of most bureaus and divisions.

Full employment goals, then, empowered the Women's Bureau to formulate policies designed to support women as permanent workers and to contest customs within the Labor Department that privileged the male breadwinner. This advocacy of women's employment rights became more pronounced in the context of the federal activism of the Kennedy and Johnson administrations, discussed in Chapters 3 and 4, which produced a political environment that freed the Women's Bureau from the posture of "bureaucratic neutrality," a position that is best illustrated by its active support of the Equal Rights Amendment after 1970.

CHAPTER I

A Blueprint for Social Change

Frieda Miller and
the Women's Economic Agenda, 1944-1953

ON APRIL 8, 1943, the *New York Times* invited twelve prominent women to comment on the theme "What Kind of World Do We Want?" The panel of writers, lawyers, educators, and government officials agreed that "we cannot return to the methods and habits of the pre-war world."[1] Women's expanded roles as citizens and workers during World War II prompted these commentators to separate the status of women into prewar and postwar categories. They hoped for a world in which women could identify permanently with the public roles they had assumed during the war emergency. Panelist Frieda Miller, who replaced Mary Anderson as director of the Women's Bureau in 1944, wished that working women be treated as individuals and not denied training because of their sex.

Women's elevated status in economic and civic life during wartime proved to be impermanent, yet the absence of real institutional change did not dampen expectations among feminist activists. Federal policies to facilitate women's employment in war industries— haphazard, temporary measures, dependent on voluntary compliance by employers—failed to protect female workers from discriminatory hiring and wage-setting practices after World War II. Unions sought to preserve prewar gains for male workers. Despite this backlash, the Women's Bureau and women's organizations, reduced to defending women's right to work in reaction to systematic discrimination against married women during the Great Depression, found a blueprint for social change in temporary equal pay and nondiscriminatory hiring policies promoted by the War Manpower Commission and the War Labor Board and equal pay clauses in union contracts. Several well-established national women's organizations, including the Business and Professional Women's Clubs, the American Association of University Women, and the National Council of Jewish Women hired full-time Washington lobbyists to push for federal attention to women's issues. In the postwar years, the Women's Bureau provided one location where a loose coalition of female government officials, union members, organizational leaders, politicians, and media professionals forged "a reconversion blueprint" anchored by the goal to pass federal and state equal pay for equal work and minimum wage legislation.

Until recently, historians discounted the work of professional feminists who sought improvements in women's legal and economic status by employing "insider tactics" that included lobbying decision makers, using palpable language to present women's issues to a mass audience, and drafting legislation.[2] Women's historians writing in the 1970s and 1980s, influenced by contemporary radical feminism that looked askance at established institutions, brought a suspicion of mainstream politics and an attention to ideological issues to the study of the war and its aftermath. They concluded that the women's movement was at a "nadir" or in the "doldrums" because married women entered the labor force in large numbers for the first time in American history without, as Karen Anderson declared, an "ideological or institutional legacy that could aid in resolving the growing contradictions in women's lives."[3] More recent scholarship finds feminist activism in postwar-era efforts for individual rights so that women could assume both domestic and nondomestic duties.[4] Lacking an innovative analysis of the sexual division of labor but committed to improving women's status as workers and citizens, postwar feminist activism "bridged" the ideological chasm of Progressive Era maternalist policies' valorization of female difference and modern feminist claims to sameness.[5] This approach to social change failed to stimulate national policy debates on women's status in the 1950s, but it did produce legislative victories in the states and maintained a coalition of mainstream women's organizations, factors contributing to the development of grassroots feminism in the 1960s.

This chapter on the Women's Bureau's response to the vicissitudes of women's workforce participation and civic responsibilities following World War II illustrates the limits and accomplishments of insider tactics in the absence of a thoroughgoing analysis of women's status in U.S. society. An institutional rather than an ideological response to the displacement of female workers from industrial jobs after World War II failed to protect women from immediate injustices in the labor market. In fact, the Women's Bureau's placement efforts channeled women into sex-typed jobs less likely to be unionized or eligible for welfare state entitlements. Still, the employment placement focus in the Labor Department, dictated by the Employment Act of 1946, the presence of married women in the labor force, and the legislative goals of outside groups drew the Women's Bureau further away from active promotion of the maternalist policies characteristic of Mary Anderson's regime.

The Women's Bureau's lack of enforcement authority goes a long way to explain the paradoxical nature of its efforts to secure employment opportunities for women in the postwar years. As this chapter will show, Bureau staffers used every means at their disposal to make the case that women wanted and deserved to keep their wartime jobs. However, their use of research and publicity to shape public opinion did little to convince employers and unions to maintain women's wartime employment gains. Moreover, no mass-based women's movement emerged to back up these efforts. The Women's Bureau's subsequent placement initiative, then, focused on recruiting women for occupations experiencing shortages in the booming consumer economy: either new, yet to be sex-typed occupations or traditional "female jobs" in the retail, clerical, and service sectors.

Employer and labor union resistance to women's presence in male-dominated jobs caused women's organizations and the Women's Bureau to emphasize the maintenance of federal equal rights policies designed to recruit women into wartime employment. A focus on rights laws cemented the Women's Bureau's relationships with outside interest groups, support essential to avoiding the budget ax. In addition, efforts to achieve state minimum wage and equal pay for equal work legislation augmented the bureau's ties to state labor departments, and federal equal pay legislation promised to expand the enforcement authority of the Labor Department. No such advantages would ensue from a campaign for the Equal Rights Amendment. While institutionalizing an equal rights ideology, the ERA would dismantle important administrative functions related to assisting state labor departments' administration of protective labor legislation and undermine any possibility to expand the Labor Department's enforcement authority in the area of wage regulation.

Postwar feminists' interest in rights legislation stems from the persistence of inequality after World War II despite women's essential role in wartime production. From the beginning of World War II, most employers, unions, and government policymakers considered women as a reserve army of laborers, and resisted their employment for as long as possible.[6] The confluence of the wartime draft and the burgeoning defense industry toppled barriers to women's employment.[7] Large numbers of women went to work in defense plants and joined industrial unions despite apathy and resistance on the part of unions and employers. The aircraft industry employed 310,000 women; 200,000 women worked in the automobile industry; wartime industries created positions for 374,000 female electrical workers.[8] Expanded employment opportunities changed the composition of the labor force dramatically. In 1945 36 percent of the female population fourteen years of age and older worked compared to 22 percent in 1940.[9] Thus, six million women entered the labor force for the first time. Married women accounted for this change, outnumbering single women in the labor force for the first time in American history.[10] Three million women joined unions during World War II, more than three times the number unionized in 1940.[11]

The Women's Bureau responded to changing workforce participation patterns by focusing on employment placement during and after World War II. Government mobilization efforts to recruit both single and married women into the labor force to replace draft-age men by 1943 prompted the Labor Department to initiate several studies on postwar employment trends. D'Ann Campbell suggests that new social science survey techniques developed during wartime, "large scale samples, personal interviews, and systematic coding," enabled government agencies to make an unparalleled evaluation of the "social and economic conditions of American women, their attitudes, behavior, and values."[12] This new research focus further supplanted the Women's Bureau's traditional studies of working conditions, which chronicled women's victimization at work, and gave Rosie the Riveter a voice when combat soldiers evinced more sympathy than homefront laborers. Despite the persistence of discriminatory promotion, hiring, and wage rates during the war, surveys showed that a significant number of women wanted to make permanent commitments to industrial work. These findings encouraged the Women's Bureau to use research and publicity to sway public opinion and convince employers and unions to voluntarily support women's economic interests. Although moral persuasion yielded few positive results, women's interest in remaining in the workforce could not be ignored in the Labor Department.

The presence of women in the industrial sector of the economy did little to challenge long-standing prejudice, as unions and employers instituted policies ensuring that women, especially married women, would not become permanent substitutes for men. The Women's Bureau's own studies proved that women generally did not receive the same opportunities to upgrade their skills as men. Employers in the heavy metal industries often placed women in jobs not in the usual line of promotion or made arbitrary promotion decisions. Foremen or shop stewards served as additional gatekeepers of this "internal labor market."[13] As a result, shipyards and the aircraft industry often kept women as "helpers" even after they passed union tests for advancement.[14] Union locals further restricted women's employment to the war emergency by manipulating seniority lists and job classifications in similar ways.[15]

Despite institutional barriers to real employment opportunities, not every woman wanted to leave lucrative skilled jobs for home and hearth. Between 1944 and 1948 war workers wrote to the Women's Bureau expressing dismay over sudden dismissals from jobs they had been performing adequately for several years. Bonnie Gutherie Smith wrote, "Women were earnestly begged to work in war plants while the war was going on and, as usual, after it is over, women are kicked out."[16] Another woman, stripped of her membership in the Oysterman's and Shrimpers Union at the end of the war, also felt frustration when labor union practices resulted in her unemployment: "If I'm not mistaken the AFL is a man's union. I joined it during the war. When they couldn't get a union to open oysters I could open oysters. The union didn't say anything about it. But now they want to stop me and I don't think it is fair."[17] Ruth Burns attributed her job reclassification to an emerging backlash against the woman worker:

> I am an average American, one of the army of women who felt like it was her duty to get in and help win this war. On Feb. 16, 1943, was ask[ed] if I would like to learn to run a large power

shear. On June 15, 1945, I was handed a slip re-classifying me to a "B" operator at 10 cents per hr. cut in pay. Only reason given was, I couldn't run any type of power shear, what's more was also told I never had been an "A" operator, and was just now being classified where I should be! I was stunned, along with all the other operators, who were all women. Part of us went to the union, results were as naught [... clas]sification.[18]

Ruth Burns's letter of comp[laint ...] job with lesser pay as the war [...] question: "What is the answer [...]

Historians agree that a w[...] not support women's claims [...] lawyers, and public relations [...] answer lay in the facts; decade[...] why women worked and how [...] policymakers and researchers [...] geneous group—single, highl[y ...] came of age after the passage [...] though a generation removed [...] these "sisters in suits," still s[...] bar, assumed professional po[...] fare institutions that their predecessors helped create.[19] As career civil servants, they had the interest and training to seek social change through expertise. Frieda Miller came to social welfare work from academia; she had an economics fellowship for three of her four years of graduate training at the University of Chicago and taught at Bryn Mawr before getting involved in the Philadelphia branch of the Women's Trade Union League. Before World War II she served as the industrial commissioner for the State of New York, the second woman to hold the post once occupied by Secretary of Labor Frances Perkins.[20]

Not club women or social workers, many of the division chiefs developed policies for other federal agencies before coming to the Women's Bureau. Chief labor economist Constance Williams, with degrees from Vassar and Simmons College, taught at Barnard and then worked at the National War Labor Board while earning a doctorate in economics from the University of Chicago, which she received in 1942 at the age of thirty-five. Margaret Plunkett, born a

Women of the WB [handwritten marginalia]

year before Williams in 1906, received a doctorate in history from Cornell University. She, too, taught at a university and worked in government before joining the Women's Bureau as a researcher in the late 1940s. Radcliffe College graduate Miriam Keeler worked in the Children's Bureau and the Bureau of Labor Standards before becoming an editor in the Publicity Division in 1951. Publicity Division chief, Mary V. Robinson, also worked at the Children's Bureau. Statistician Mildred Barber, who did postgraduate work at the Boston College School of Law, Harvard, and Northeastern University, came from the War Labor Board. Chief of the postwar Employment Opportunities Section, Marguerite Zapoleon, one of the few married women on the staff, had worked as an occupational specialist for the District of Columbia.[21]

Armed with research data, Miller and her colleagues claimed expertise on the future employment outlook and stated emphatically that women were in the labor force to stay. The Women's Bureau's study, "Women Workers in Ten War Production Areas and Their Postwar Employment Plans," found that 80 percent of women working in war industries wanted to stay in their jobs, although those under thirty-five years old who had previously labored at home planned to return there.[22] The Publicity Division used the study to argue that, despite the voluntary movement of some swing-shift Susies out of the labor market, women in manufacturing would increase beyond 1940 levels. Frieda Miller stressed this point in her interview with the *New York Times* about the Buffalo findings, stating that "9 out of 10 of those employed in the area help support families."[23] *June 16, 1945 p 16* [handwritten marginalia]

Public appearances, press releases, and popular articles resonated with the theme that women deserved equal consideration when it came to seniority status, union membership, and promotions because families depended on their wages. Collaboration between female professionals in the federal government and the news media kept swing-shift Susie on the front page, or at least on the "style" pages. Representatives from the Association of Women Broadcasters and the Women's National Press Club participated in Women's Bureau–sponsored reconversion conferences, for example. Conversely, Frieda Miller spoke at their conferences. Personal ties did make a difference. Research projects analyzing union contracts and employers' hiring policies received regular coverage in the *New*

York Times, in part thanks to division chief Mary Robinson's efforts to win reporter Bess Furman's good will.[24] Two articles signed by Frieda Miller, "What Has Become of Rosie the Riveter" and "Help Wanted—Women?" appeared in the *New York Times Magazine* in 1945 and 1946 respectively. Female radio broadcasters became part of this public relations dynamo as well. Miller appeared as a guest commentator on twenty-two female-hosted radio programs in 1945 alone, such as Ruth Crane's "women's show" on WMAL in Washington, D.C.[25]

Between 1944 and 1946, staffers penned articles for a number of national news and entertainment magazines, including *Look, Newsweek,* the *New Leader, American Mercury, Tomorrow,* and *Predictions,* on the topic of women in the postwar labor market. Several articles appeared in women's magazines aimed at younger readers, such as *Glamour, Charm,* and *Junior Bazaar.* In fact, *Glamour* made frequent requests for editorial assistance and contributions to its monthly career column.[26] These soapboxes amplified assessments of female workers' aspirations and goals.

Analyses of union contracts also became grist for the public relations mill. Publications argued consistently that female workers fared better when "industrial sisters" counted among unions' national and local leadership. An article by Frieda Miller in the *Trade Union Courier* related the data from the Women's Bureau's 1946 "Union Study" to prove that union contracts created separate job classifications for men and women despite claims by national union officers to the contrary. To remedy this situation, Miller suggested that negotiators incorporate into contracts procedures guaranteeing equal opportunities for promotion and training and equal pay for equal work provisions.[27] A 1945 Women's Bureau publication on seniority guidelines in union shops reported that locals impeded the progressive goals of the trade union movement by supporting contract clauses discriminating against married women.[28]

Both through voluntary quits or forced displacement of female workers, the sex-segregated labor market returned with a vengeance after World War II despite the Women's Bureau's efforts to shape public opinion. Pink slips greeted the Susies and Rosies during the summer months of 1945, as one out of every four women lost factory jobs.[29] The number of women employed in the automobile industry plummeted to more than half of wartime numbers to

134,000 from 280,000. Even before the end of the war, employers in Detroit laid off female workers at the end of government contracts, and these women found it difficult to get other industrial jobs.[30] Federal requirements that employers rehire returning veterans further undermined women's seniority status. As a result, women's labor union membership fell off precipitously, especially in prewar male-dominated unions, which lost 43 percent of their female membership.[31] D'Ann Campbell notes that Frieda Miller testified before Congress in 1948 "that management and unions alike had refused to give women an equal opportunity for supplemental training, upgrading, and supervisory work."[32]

Women's Bureau staffers quietly pressured bureaus and divisions within the federal government not to institutionalize this backlash against women workers. Karen Anderson found a propensity in the United States Employment Service (USES) to channel both men and women into suitable gender-typed work. The employment service in Detroit denied unemployment benefits to women who refused to consider clerical or retail jobs and discouraged men who had gained clerical experience during the war from applying for white-collar work instead of seeking placement in manufacturing.[33] Miller, aware that employment security workers ignored "the rights of women workers to benefits," urged Bureau of Employment Security Director Ewan Clague to analyze the effects of peacetime displacement.[34] The Women's Bureau tried to change USES's discriminatory practices behind the scenes by using its authority to select the female members of its advisory board and assigning Marguerite Zapoleon as liaison officer.[35]

Labor economists on the staff, Alice Angus and Mary Elizabeth Pigeon, met with Bureau of Labor Statistics (BLS) employees to persuade them to include surveys of wages in occupations dominated by women, which they argued were often left out of compilations of wage data.[36] In 1946, they urged the BLS to compile current data on the contributions women made to family incomes, especially as sole supporters.[37] Two years later, Miller, with the encouragement of labor union women attending a Women's Bureau–sponsored reconversion conference, entreated the industrial relations section of the BLS to include equal pay, nondiscrimination, and promotion in agency analyses of collective bargaining agreements.[38]

Bureau staffers worked tirelessly to ensure that the Labor Department's full employment policies defined women as full-time workers. The Employment Act of 1946, establishing the President's Council of Economic Advisors (CEA) and Congress's Joint Economic Committee, directed Labor Department divisions and bureaus to concentrate on labor forecasting.[39] As it gained administrative tasks associated with becoming a centralized and more prominent clearinghouse for employment data, the Labor Department moved away from worker advocacy toward pragmatic manpower planning. New labor force forecasting projects generated a flurry of memo writing between the Women's Bureau and the Bureau of Labor Statistics. Constance Williams criticized the BLS's emphasis on the female wage earner who supplemented her mate's income.[40] She wanted statisticians to correct this perspective by studying plants in which men and women engaged in comparable employment.[41]

Ironically, the Women's Bureau countered the lingering stereotype that women did not make full-time, permanent commitments to work with a different gender stereotype. Its newly established Employment Opportunities Section within the Research Division steered women into occupations created by the consumer economy, occupations that lacked incentives for advancement and the benefits of unionization. Staff member Kathryn Blood's article in *Glamour* urged women to consider employment options outside of the industrial sector: "If you've been a Swing-shift Susie and love it, you may be able to continue to weld—burr—rivet—drill—shape—form—draft—out—hobb—grind—polish—your own living in one of the lighter consumer industries."[42] Although it suggested that some women would remain in shipbuilding and aircraft industries in a strong economy, the article stressed that most women were "nonmechanical Nells" who voluntarily left wartime work for employment "in which they could use their characteristic abilities."[43] These occupations included assembling small articles, inspecting, wrapping, and packing. Moreover, the "sweet girl graduate of high school" could pursue a career in human welfare occupations as a nurse, teacher, hospital administrator, medical technician, physical or occupational therapist, or social worker.[44]

The bureau's occupational bulletin series publicized female-dominated white-collar jobs and ignored blue-collar jobs and male-dominated professions that war workers, not inclined to turn into "non-mechanical Nells" at the stroke of midnight, wanted to retain. For example, the series on medical fields accentuated occupations already dominated by women, such as medical laboratory technicians, practical nurses, and dental hygienists. On the other hand, the bulletin on physicians noted the small percentage of women in the field and the existence of discrimination, particularly for female physicians wishing to affiliate with hospitals. Although it conceded that women could be found in all specialties, the bulletin nevertheless predicted that the specialties of psychiatry, pediatrics, and public health would remain the most popular choices.[45] A series on scientific occupations, published in 1947, projected openings for those job seekers with training in chemistry in low-paying gender-typed jobs as teachers, medical technicians, and librarians.[46]

By today's standards, these research projects and publicity campaigns lamely criticize blatant sexism, and an adherence to the sex-segregated labor market seems anachronistic; however, the Women's Bureau's investigations into women's displacement from the most desirable jobs and attendant public relations efforts pleading for fairness and equity are significant in the pre-civil rights era and in the absence of a mass-based women's rights movement. The well-established research and publicity divisions used survey data to make a public case that women wanted to remain in industrial jobs after World War II. Studies on women's postwar plans bolstered the Women's Bureau's fight within the Labor Department to include women in post–World War II full employment policies. More important, the 1946 Employment Act enabled the Women's Bureau to initiate a separate placement initiative that recognized married women's commitment to full-time work.

Even so, placement efforts centering on low-paying female-dominated occupations did little to address the needs of a new breed of female worker: an older woman with children less interested in protection from working conditions than in adequate wages and benefits. Paychecks determined benefit levels in welfare state entitlements such as Social Security and workers' compensation. Moreover, women working in small service concerns not engaged in interstate commerce failed to qualify for federal minimum wage protection. Service workers such as Mrs. P. W. Sikes, a theater worker from Levelland, Texas, wrote to the Women's

Bureau seeking advice on how to increase wages: "I am writing for a group of women workers of the local theaters. They do not belong to any union but want to find out if they could demand and get a raise in salary."[47] Rather than suggest to Mrs. Sikes that she and her friends consider preparing for positions in higher-paying fields or join a union, Miller gave this advice: "You might also care to add your support to that of many other low-paid workers in Texas toward getting a state minimum wage law passed in the next session of your legislature."[48] Why rely on the state?

The minimum wage and equal pay bills drafted by the Women's Bureau represent attempts to extend bureaucratic authority through exercises in policy formation. The administration of state and federal labor laws required teams of experts to assess methods of enforcement. Historically, minimum wage laws covering women included the establishment of minimum wage boards to determine adequate living standards. State labor bureaus often created women's divisions to oversee this and other administrative aspects of protective labor legislation. These sex-segregated divisions, in turn, depended on the Women's Bureau's living standards and occupational distribution studies for enforcement of state wage laws. This administrative interdependency thwarted Frances Perkins's efforts to subsume the Women's Bureau's program under the mission of the Bureau of Labor Standards in 1934 after she failed to combine the Women's and Children's Bureaus in 1933.[49] The possibility of expanded administrative authority, in addition to the fact that women outnumbered men in occupations engaged in intrastate commerce, explains the Women's Bureau's persistent commitment to minimum wage laws covering women as a separate class of worker.

Passage of equal pay legislation, within reach at the end of World War II, also promised to augment bureaucratic authority. The Women's Bureau inherited equal pay policies from the Women in Industry Service, a federal agency established during World War I to mobilize women for war work, which encouraged the National War Labor Board to actively enforce equal pay requirements in war production. As the permanent federal agency to represent female workers replacing the Women in Industry Service, the Women's Bureau did not pursue equal pay legislation in the 1920s and 1930s because court rulings restricting federal authority over the workplace precluded bids to legislate wage regulation until the New

Deal era. The execution of equal pay policies in war industries by the National War Labor Board during World War II and a judicial climate favorable to federal regulatory powers—thanks to President Franklin Delano Roosevelt's appointment of new Supreme Court justices—put equal pay back on the Women's Bureau's agenda. During World War II Mary Anderson praised the policy as an important step toward setting equal wages regardless of sex. The economist Constance Williams and the statistician Mildred Barber, equal pay policymakers with the World War II National War Labor Board, moved to the Women's Bureau during Miller's tenure. The historian Margaret Plunkett, who served on the War Production Board, also joined the staff. These war agency bureaucrats contributed to drafting equal pay agency bills in later years.

The bills drafted by the Women's Bureau—S. 1178, The Women's Equal Pay Act of 1945, known as the Morse-Pepper bill, and similar legislation proposed in the House of Representatives, H.R. 5221, introduced by Connecticut Republican Chase Going Woodhouse—vested administrative authority in the Labor Department. Essentially, the draft bills defined unequal wage rates as an unfair labor practice and empowered the Labor Department to pursue remedial action through litigation. Section Three of the Morse-Pepper bill created an equal pay division within the Women's Bureau with investigatory powers and authorized hiring additional employees under civil service laws for that division. More important, the bill greatly enhanced the power of the Women's Bureau director, who could recommend legal action to the attorney general, rescind rules and regulations, and authorize expenditures necessary to pursue enforcement of the act.[50] The House version also contained the equal pay division for the Women's Bureau. Even though Frieda Miller testified at congressional hearings that equal pay bills in no way set wage rates for employers, it was equally clear that a much more complex administrative system would be necessary to ensure compliance.[51] The enforcement powers provided in postwar equal pay proposals promised an astounding expansion of federal authority, all within an agency fighting constantly to stay open for business.

Unions, still a primary Labor Department constituency, supported equal pay policy formation, albeit for different reasons. Unions applied federal policies establishing the principle of equal pay for equal work to prevent employers from using women to depress wages in "men's jobs" during World War II and sought to codify these policies after the war to prevent employers from hiring women to replace men. The United Automobile, Aircraft, and Agricultural Workers of America (UAW) and United Electrical Workers (UE) unions not only supported federal equal pay policies during wartime to protect prewar gains for male workers but also as a means to secure wage increases during the government's wage freeze.[52] Both unions took unequal wage complaints against employers to the War Labor Board, which approved wage increases for women who labored in "men's jobs."[53] Although Congress failed to pass equal pay legislation, laws passed in states with a significant industrial labor force during the war years and shortly thereafter, including New York, Michigan, and Illinois. This legislation had the practical effect of covering one-quarter of female wage earners.[54]

Women's organizations adopted equal pay for equal work policies as the best way to ensure workplace equity. As Susan Levine argues in her history of the American Association of University Women, "mainstream national women's organizations (including AAUW) did not disappear, become silent concerning gender-based discrimination, or abandon their interest in broad-based social reform after suffrage, nor did they 'rediscover' feminism during the 1960s."[55] Yet, she adds that postwar conservatism required "changing organizational and political strategies, and shifts in the language used to describe women's aims."[56] Women's organizations made institutional commitments to insider tactics and avoided political conflicts with anti-feminists and cold warriors. Consequently, institutionalizing wartime policies became the most prominent political goal of several women's organizations. According to Susan Lynn, the YWCA's 1945 Public Affairs Program's promotion of equal pay for equal work legislation demonstrates that "in the area of women's labor force participation, the YWCA formulated feminist positions that recognized the existence of male supremacy and sought to end it."[57] The BPW, AAUW, and NCJW hired professional Washington lobbyists for the first time after World War II.

Professional feminist activists joined federal bureaucrats in forming a core group of full-time policy advocates. While young women—high school and college graduates in the 1940s—embraced domestic roles in large numbers after the war, either voluntarily or in response to a lack of choice offered in the postwar labor market, professional activists in women's organizations, unions, and state and federal governments of a previous generation, more inspired by the New Deal than the "suburban ideal," continued to work for social change. Social welfare professionals and organizational leaders aspired to involvement in mainstream politics, especially policy formation in the welfare state. The professional staff of several women's organizations sustained feminist activism over time. In addition to the politically active BPW and AAUW, the YWCA, League of Women Voters, National Council of Catholic Women, and NCJW supported a national headquarters and a professional staff, published newsletters and magazines, and held national and regional conferences. Organizational professionals responsible for these functions maintained interest in women's issues among state branches.

Marguerite Rawalt's career illustrates the hopes and concerns of this generation. Rawalt succeeded in getting a law degree in the 1930s after being turned away from admission to Georgetown Law School in 1929. She kept her married status a secret for three years in order to keep her job with the Internal Revenue Service in the wake of Section 213 of the 1932 Economy Act prohibiting married spouses from working for the federal government. Wartime opportunities gave Rawalt choices she heretofore did not have. In 1943 she became the first female president of the Federal Bar Association, joined the BPW while attending a White House conference presided over by Eleanor Roosevelt, and signed on with the National Woman's Party. Denied professional opportunities after the war, Rawalt applied her professional training to full-time activist work—she became president of the BPW in 1956.[58]

Female trade unionists joined this emerging postwar coalition of professional feminists. The influx of women to the industrial labor force after 1943 changed the internal politics of labor unions. In both the UAW and UE women replaced men as business agents, shop stewards, and even local presidents. Work stoppages also schooled women in public activism: 39 percent of the strikes in 1944 included both men and women.[59] Nancy Gabin has shown how discriminatory reconversion policies stimulated a feminist sensibility among UAW women leaders: "As a result of the war and reconversion some union women began to advocate equal rather than differential treatment as the appropriate strategy for obtaining gender equality in the work-place."[60] Although reconversion thinned the female rank and file by instituting a return of the sex-segregated labor force, UAW feminists had enough clout during the union's 1946 national convention to create a feminist organization within the union, the UAW Women's Bureau. Equal pay for equal work legislation, already part of the union's political agenda, became one of the UAW Women's Bureau's postwar goals. During both world wars trade unions embraced equal pay proposals to prevent women from replacing men, but by the 1940s, with the return of the sex-segregated labor market, women promoted equal pay for comparable work legislative language to raise wages in feminized occupations.[61]

The UAW Women's Bureau functioned as a feminist institution in much the same way as its federal counterpart and moderate women's organizations, with which it joined in coalitions to work for equal rights policies. UAW Women's Bureau director Mildred Jeffrey's career paralleled that of professional feminists in government and women's organizations. Well educated, with degrees from Bryn Mawr and the University of Minnesota, Jeffrey, too, was employed in the federal government during World War II. She sought employment within the trade union movement when professional opportunities for women dissipated after World War II.[62] The UAW Women's Bureau also stimulated activism by establishing advisory committees, holding regional women's conferences, and publishing informational newsletters.[63] In fact, Gladys Dickason, vice president and research director of the Amalgamated Clothing Workers of America and assistant chairman of the Congress of Industrial Organizations (CIO) Committee for the Organization of the South, explained in 1947 that unions were the working-class equivalent of a women's civic or service club: "Working-class women do not as a rule belong to the Red Cross, women's clubs, and similar community organizations to which leisured middle-class women belong, unless the union provides an opportunity for them to participate."[64] In other words, unions provided a location for the political education of women, a place where they could initiate community projects, get involved in union elections, and fight for increased social services.

Women's organizations and labor unions with large national memberships and strong state and local branches became prominent policy partners for promotion of federal and state legislation. The Women's Bureau provided expertise, public relations connections, and national networks to state labor departments, especially women's divisions, which, in turn, executed policy goals developed on the federal level. Women's organizations entered into this policy matrix; state branches formed coalitions with state labor departments while national bodies, representing millions of women, commanded the resources necessary to put political pressure on Congress. The Women's Bureau welcomed and courted organizations it considered to be "action oriented."[65] For example, to accommodate the BPW's criticism that the Women's Bureau placed too much emphasis on protective labor legislation, Miller created a new division, Labor Legislation and Civil and Political Status, to aid women's organizations interested in challenging discriminatory customs in state and federal law. The new division drafted state jury legislation and two federal jury bills, S. 18 and H.R. 3214, to end discrimination against women in jury selection, in cooperation with the AAUW's National Committee on the Status of Women and the BPW's Legislative Steering Committee.[66]

On the other hand, two organizations committed to pursuing protective labor legislation for women during the 1920s and 1930s, the Women's Trade Union League and the National Consumers' League (NCL), floundered once their social welfare agendas became part of the New Deal, and as a consequence, lost influence over policy formation. The National Women's Trade Union League disbanded in 1950, citing the strength of the American Federation of Labor (AFL) and CIO unions in diminishing the need for a separate group to carry out educational and legislative work in the labor field.[67] Whereas the NCL, always an elite organization with a small membership, not only lacked the state branches necessary to lobby for wage legislation in the states but also emphasized a program to improve working conditions for migratory workers. However, the National Consumers' League enabled former Women's Bureau director Mary Anderson to remain politically connected as the league's representative on the Women's Joint Congressional Committee and the Committee to Defeat the Unequal Rights Amendment.

Women's Bureau–sponsored national conferences on the postwar status of women between 1944 and 1946 secured an extensive

[handwritten margin notes: WB conference; would coalition; + networks]

policy network in the public and private sectors. Two of these meetings brought together national women's organizations and female
government bureaucrats and media professionals, and two conferences organized labor union women exclusively. The first conference,
"Postwar Adjustments of Women Workers," drew representatives
from thirty national women's organizations, although equal rights
feminists from the National Woman's Party opposed to any sex-
based labor legislation did not receive an invitation from the Labor
Department. Female representatives from state and federal governments and personnel directors rounded out the participant list.
Frieda Miller urged participants to use the research papers on wage
legislation and the postwar employment outlook presented at the
conference for pedagogical activism: "Carry on an extensive program educating women themselves, labor groups, employers, and the
general public, as to the social and economic significance of women
as workers."[68]

In addition to a joint commitment to initiate antibacklash publicity, the conference developed action items in a "Reconversion Blueprint," which incorporated the Labor Department's postwar emphasis on employment placement and legislative remedies for low wages
in sex-typed jobs. The following Blueprint recommendations formed
the basis of a political coalition in the absence of a mass-based feminist movement: "establishment of anti-discrimination policies, sufficient public employment service facilities, training and re-training
facilities, the advance planning of public works programs; and the
extension to all states of the collective bargaining, minimum wage
and equal pay for equal work laws."[69] National representatives
offered to promote the Blueprint through federal, state, and local
governmental systems. They also agreed to seek inclusion on local
community planning boards and to supplement the work of community employment agencies and counseling agencies. On the regional
level, organizations planned conferences in order to build cooperative networks in the states.

A 1945 reconversion conference for labor union women developed a similar action plan that focused on empowering working women through pedagogical and political activism. Union
leaders pledged to educate women about union procedures, seniority principles, and grievance procedures, so they could "put up
a fight to eliminate discrimination against women wherever it

exists."[70] Leadership goals extended into community activism with commitments to become members of government agencies and community planning groups and to create public services for women. Policy recommendations supported the Reconversion Blueprint, including a charge to the Women's Bureau to aid unions in establishing labor legislation by furnishing data, writing drafts of minimum wage bills, and writing briefs if labor legislation was challenged in the courts.

In addition to sponsoring conferences, Miller and her staff of regional representatives made public appearances at national conferences and local meetings of women's organizations obliged to pursue the Reconversion Blueprint in the states. For example, Miller attended BPW conferences on the "Postwar Problems of Service Women" and on equal pay.[71] National organizations created special committees on reconversion issues and held conferences on that topic. Bureau regional offices in the major metropolitan areas of Boston, New York, Chicago, San Francisco, Philadelphia, and St. Louis maintained Blueprint organization in the states and local communities. The presence of federal officials at these regional and national conferences influenced organizational goals and changed attitudes, as is evident in Helen Mills's thank-you letter to Miller for attending the Michigan AAUW's reconversion conference: "Many people spoke about their understanding for the first time of the reasons for women needing to go out into the community even where there was not a question of financial necessity. So you must have sold a real bill of goods. Certainly you added much to the thinking on the problems of women in business and industry."[72]

The Women's Bureau's bulletin, "Negro Women War Workers," generated requests from black women's organizations for public appearances and additional information as well, but Miller kept a low profile to avoid alienating southern branches of activist white women's organizations, particularly the AAUW and BPW. When Miller was in Memphis, Tennessee, at the request of the local AAUW, she met "off the record" with an interracial group at the YWCA. Mrs. Jasspon of the AAUW first suggested an off-the-record meeting with the interracial group, and Miller concurred: "I do agree with you that this would be more useful off the record than on it and would prefer to keep it so."[73] Lower-ranking staff member Kathryn Blood served as an unofficial liaison between the

Women's Bureau and African American organizations. She gave a talk on women in the postwar economy before the National Negro Congress Postwar Conference on January 13, 1945, and served on an employment panel sponsored by the National Council of Negro Women in 1947.[74]

The Women's Bureau maintained the coalitions built during national conferences by forming advisory committees of labor union women and representatives from national women's organizations, including the NCNW. These advisory committees in turn contributed to the development of research and publicity projects and policy formation within the Women's Bureau into the 1950s. In addition to the aforementioned jury service and wage regulation bills, advisory committees advocated and helped to draft federal legislation extending Social Security benefits, a maternity leave bill for married women in the federal service, amendments to the Internal Revenue Code to permit working women to deduct child care expenses, and legislation to equalize immigration laws.[75] The policy partners also initiated efforts to ensure equity in family law, particularly in divorce and child guardianship.[76] In some cases advisory committees established independent feminist agendas that challenged the Women's Bureau's traditional mission. Most notably, the Trade Union Advisory Committee urged the Women's Bureau to initiate a study of existing state laws restricting night work. Mildred Jeffrey from the UAW remarked during an advisory committee meeting in 1946 that "after the hard work of establishing job rights for women, it was very difficult to have a night work law to contend with—that if women could not be on the 2nd shift then all women would probably be out of jobs."[77]

Surveys of hotel and restaurant workers, also done at the behest of the trade union group, likewise potentially served as a basis for a policy shift within the Women's Bureau. Constance Williams's outline of the study excluded questions considering the women's health and focused on the influence of existing night work prohibitions on promotions and wages and on women's attitudes toward this type of labor legislation. She argued in a memo to Miller that if the data revealed that "night work decreased employment opportunities or decreased wages . . . it would be reasonable for us to take a position that we did not think that legislation prohibiting night work by women was desirable."[78] Williams's pronouncement notwithstanding, staffers considered the policy implications of the study very carefully. A confidential internal memo listed the pros and cons of abandoning night work restrictions as a policy goal. Even though the Women's Bureau abandoned efforts to pass night work laws, the memo raised questions about the outcome of a public reversal on night work restrictions: "Would a move to eliminate existing night work regulations start the toboggan toward eliminating other and far more vital labor standards, and thus be likely to affect a very great number of precisely those workers who are in the weakest position in bargaining for improvement of their conditions of work?"[79]

Surveys of service workers' attitudes toward night work restrictions undertaken from 1946 to 1948, taking into account regional and population diversity—20 cities and towns in all—produced conflicting evidence. Some women reported that night work posed hardships, while others found the hours convenient. The researchers found that "many women now need to work at night, so that their days can be open for family and household responsibilities."[80] The absence of strong preferences either for or against night work laws justified making such legislation a low priority but precluded a call to repeal existing night work laws. Instead, the Research Division produced an equivocal report recommending that "better community services for their convenience would provide greater freedom to accept day-time employment."[81] The response to the night work policy is quintessential bureaucratic behavior. Rather than publicly change a policy, which might affect other programs, the bureau quietly cast aside active promotion of night work legislation and suggested alternative policies.

With night work research studies in hand, the Trade Union Advisory Committee released a position paper on the issue in 1949, concluding that night work legislation no longer fit women's needs or conditions in the workforce. The report noted that night work prohibitions to safeguard health "did not exist today" and that social custom prevented the elimination of all night work.[82] An acknowledgment that night work laws represented a state response to industrial conditions in another era notwithstanding, the committee still stated that evening work for women remained "socially undesirable."[83] The justification for continued advocacy of night work restrictions shifted from a concern with women's health to a matter of control of the workplace: "It is the belief of the Committee that in the United States women's legislation has helped to restrict night work, especially in manufacturing industries where there is no inherent need for continuous process, and that this means of control should be supported and bolstered."[84]

The Women's Bureau's accommodation to feminist politics within women's organizations and trade union groups maintained a coalition of outside pressure groups that saved it as a separate agency within the Labor Department. In 1947 the "meat-ax" Eightieth Congress, controlled by Republicans after the 1946 elections, reported a Labor Department appropriations bill out of the House Appropriations Subcommittee that did not fund the Women's Bureau.[85] Secretary of Labor Lewis B. Schwellenbach let the cut stand. The stunning budget developments in 1947 caught the Women's Bureau by surprise. Frieda Miller, attending an International Labor Organization conference in Geneva, Switzerland, left deputy director Anne Larrabee to muster political support inside and outside of the Labor Department. In a February 14 letter to Miller relating the trouble brewing in Washington, Larrabee confessed that she "didn't feel much like a valentine" after a Monday afternoon meeting in which she heard that the "Labor Department had its back against the wall as far as appropriations were concerned."[86] Secretary Schwellenbach's congressional liaison, May Thompson Evans, who happened to be a Bureau backer, confided to Larrabee that the men, assuming that the Women's Bureau could mobilize outside support, chose to focus on saving Labor Standards from elimination.[87] Indeed, Schwellenbach told Larrabee that "women would make such a fuss that the men on the Hill wouldn't dare cut it out completely."[88] Larrabee knew that the men struck a backroom deal with Labor Standards: "I went up to see Johnson again and played dumb—I want him to think I don't know they have a deal with L.S. [Labor Standards]. . . . He called me honey and said not to worry—everything would be all right—the double crossing so and so."[89]

Schwellenbach told Larrabee not to call Miller back from Europe, but the intrepid deputy ignored this directive and in a diplomatic way tried to convince Miller that the situation required her presence. Additional pleas to Miller to return to the office followed. Sylvia Beyer, on the staff of the Publicity Division, wrote to Miller:

"The Bureau's staff with its seriousness of purpose can live without music but is entitled to have its spirits lifted by a note or two from its bugler. I'm *not* advising you to fly—I love and value you too much. But I'd certainly pick me a berth fast and wouldn't wait for a luxury liner."[90] Beyer also shared her analysis of the budget problems, reckoning that the Republicans wanted to disband programs and then restore services in 1948 with their own personnel, which, she admitted, would be a difficult thing to fight.

House Appropriations Subcommittee chairman Frank B. Keefe, a Republican from Wisconsin, had expressed animus toward the Women's Bureau, stating publicly that women in his district had never heard of it and that "pet projects and favorite little bureaus would have to be abandoned in line with the economy program."[91] Larrabee assumed that he had talked with "rural Catholic women."[92] During appropriations hearings, Keefe placed a statement into the *Congressional Record* reiterating his commitment to standing up to "propaganda mills and propaganda agencies" in order to "balance the budget and lay something aside for a rainy day."[93]

Lucky for the Women's Bureau, powerful women in both the Democratic and Republican parties had heard of its activities and pledged support. The Women's Joint Congressional Committee's (WJCC) Subcommittee on Women's Bureau Appropriations led the effort to mobilize women's organizations.[94] The WJCC subcommittee included professional lobbyists from national women's organizations in constant contact with the Women's Bureau, including the National Council of Jewish Women's Olya Margolin, Elizabeth Christman of the Women's Trade Union League, and Geneva Mcquartters of the BPW.[95] These political insiders organized a letter-writing campaign to Representative Keefe and other members of the subcommittee and enlisted state branches of national women's groups to work in each member's district. Female members of Congress also joined the fight. Larrabee reported to Miller that Chase Going Woodhouse was very "disturbed" by her colleague's tirade against the bureau and offered to "do anything she can."[96]

The political pressure worked. At the December 8 meeting of the WJCC, Elizabeth Christman cheerfully reported that Chairman Keefe had complained to a *Washington Post* reporter that newspaper coverage of the budget controversy "got all the women on my neck."[97] Even in the absence of Frieda Miller, who did not return in time to testify, the House subcommittee voted a $263,000 appropriation for the Women's Bureau. To save face, however, the subcommittee refused to grant the original budget request of $300,600 submitted to Congress from the Labor Department for automatic pay increases, not authorizing a penny more than the previous year's budget. Still, when the status quo budget survived appropriations committees from both Houses, the WJCC claimed victory because coveted programs stayed intact.[98]

Programmatic adjustments and strategic alliances that proved essential to surviving budget battles mitigated the Women's Bureau's traditional advocacy of sexual difference arguments based on assumptions of female inferiority. The bureau's postwar analysis of the persistence of unequal wage rates represents ideological adjustments that custom, not women's inability to perform adequately, accounted for discrimination. This new analysis reasoned that industrial technologies, by eliminating the need for physical strength and endurance, enabled women to be just as productive as men. In fact, sophisticated machines requiring manual dexterity and quickness made women more productive than men. Therefore, as equal or better partners in productivity, women deserved the same wages as male industrial workers.[99]

Ideological fine-tuning, changing employment patterns, the emerging employment placement focus within the Labor Department, and alliances with women's rights organizations still did not budge the anti-ERA orientation of the Women's Bureau, however; it rejected any alliance with the equal rights feminists in the National Woman's Party. Frieda Miller, a single professional woman and self-described "highbrow," actually had more in common with NWP members than with her predecessor Mary Anderson.[100] Nonetheless, she described the NWP as "a small but militant group of leisure class women that has given voice to their resentment at not having been born men by loudly proclaiming that men and women are 'equal,'" and as "women of property with conservative economic ideas," themselves out of touch with "women of the laboring people."[101] Undoubtedly, Miller believed herself to be more in touch with laboring people through her organizational affiliations and lifelong companionship with labor organizer Pauline Newman, who represented the International Ladies Garment Workers Union on the Trade Union Advisory Committee.[102]

Clearly, high political stakes inspired these and other pro-nouncements about the NWP's motivations. The "women of prop-erty" with ties to the Republican Party threatened policy formation aimed at strengthening the Labor Department. It is important to restate here that equal pay bills would have expanded the Labor Department's regulatory powers. The ERA offered no such admin-istrative foothold. In this context, the ERA represented a tool used by employers' groups to take the government out of the business of wage and hours regulation. Secretary of Labor Frances Perkins testified before Congress in 1945 that the Equal Rights Amendment would not protect women from exploitation by private employers. Rather, such a measure would jeopardize the Women's Bureau's efforts to redress the imbalance of women's wages and benefits and to provide employment opportunities.[103] Frieda Miller argued that the proposed amendment would not result in any real gains for working women: "It will not give jobs to women where employers feel it to their self interest to replace women with men. When pro-ponents claim that the Amendment will increase job opportunities for women, they hold out a promise incapable of fulfillment—an empty promise."[104]

Arguments against the ERA continued to reflect Mary Ander-son's distinction between "doctrinaire equality" and "social justice."[105] The Women's Bureau and its allies, with the notable exception of the BPW and the General Federation of Women's Clubs, accepted cod-ification of sexual difference as economically responsible in the wel-fare state. For instance, according to amendment foes, identical-age provisions for Social Security benefits affected women adversely be-cause the "majority of wives are younger than their husbands, and unless a widow has small children she is compelled to wait perhaps several years for benefits."[106] They also cited evidence that women's wage levels rose in those states with minimum wage laws. Social jus-tice would be achieved, then, through wage regulation for workers in intrastate commerce and adjustments of federal entitlements to ac-commodate women as a group.

The Committee to Defeat the Unequal Rights Amendment, func-tioning as a political adjunct to the Women's Bureau, organized opposition to the Equal Rights Amendment in Congress. Freed from her job in the federal government, Mary Anderson became treasurer of the lobbying group formed in 1944, the same year as her retirement. Dorothy McAllistor of the National Consumers' League served as president. Representatives at the inaugural meeting expressed concern that no representatives from black women's organizations were present and organized a subcommittee to inform black women about the implications of the ERA, although Mary McLeod Bethune, president of the National Council of Negro Women, wanted to study the question before committing to the antiamendment crusade. The umbrella body pressed national women's organizations to enlist state and local branch members to buttonhole senators and representatives in their home states. Of course, the Women's Bureau, represented at early meetings by Frieda Miller, provided research data illustrating what legislation would be lost through the amendment as well as studies on its limitations. However, the Women's Bureau also documented the existence of discriminatory legislation that needed to be remedied. From the beginning, the committee emphasized positive steps to abolish discrimination against women; several representatives insisted on the antidiscrimination tack.[107]

Frieda Miller used the NWP and the proposed ERA to argue that the Women's Bureau must be maintained as a separate federal agency. In 1945, Miller opposed Frances Perkins's planned consolidation of the Women's Bureau and the Bureau of Labor Standards, because "Women's Bureau activities are necessary to counteract the extremist feminist group who seeks to nourish grievances and create sex antagonisms."[108] She also stressed to Perkins the importance of informing public opinion about the potential of the ERA to nullify state protective labor legislation, which "would retard progress made toward the removal of discriminatory industrial practices."[109]

The National Woman's Party argued that any policy indicating sexual difference must be exclusionary, whereas the Women's Bureau differentiated between regulatory and discriminatory legislation and made sexual difference an acceptable criterion for employment placement. These conflicting interpretations on sexual difference informed the purpose of the Legal Status of Women Bill of 1947, to "study and review the economic, civil, political and social status of women and the extent of discriminations based on sex."[110] It is hardly a coincidence that the bill drafted by the Women's Bureau and the National Committee on the Status of Women, formerly the Committee to Defeat the Unequal Rights Amendment, expanded the bureau's mission and institutionalized its networks with state labor departments and women's organizations. Frieda Miller argued that such a commission would work with the states to amend discriminatory state laws and that women's organizations "who will carry on the fight for remedial action will find the Commission's report a potent instrument for their campaign."[111] The status bill followed a failed attempt by the committee to get congressional support for a draft joint resolution on women's status as a positive alternative to the ERA. The proposed resolution included several planks instructing Congress and the president to make commitments to equality: it required all federal agencies to review regulations and practices, provided for the appointment of a presidential commission to evaluate laws that might be discriminatory, and empowered the president to recommend additional legislation to Congress to ensure consistent antidiscrimination policies.[112] The joint resolution proposal served as a model not only for the 1947 bill but also for President John F. Kennedy's Commission on the Status of Women formed in 1961.

The Reconversion Blueprint faded on the federal level as Congress refused to enact most progressive legislation. Not only did the Women's Bureau's agency bills meet stiff opposition in Congress, but equal rights feminists and the labor movement also failed to achieve political goals. The lack of timely federal equity legislation frustrated the BPW. Even though the BPW worked closely with the Women's Bureau to get equal pay by executive order in industries working under federal contract during the Korean War, Sarah Hughes, National BPW President in 1951, began to reevaluate that alliance. Hughes and BPW legislative coordinator Marjorie Temple shared a perspective that equal pay bills failed to pass in Congress after World War II because employers objected to enforcement authority placed in the Women's Bureau. A BPW draft bill attached equal pay enforcement to the Fair Labor Standards Act, thereby undermining the Labor Department's administrative authority. Hughes hoped to spearhead an independent campaign for the more employer-friendly legislation.[113]

The Women's Bureau's 1952 Equal Pay Conference maintained the original coalition and stymied BPW efforts to initiate an independent movement. The BPW could not compete with the institutions, such as conferences, advisory committees, publications, and state coalitions with labor departments, created by the federal government. Although still committed to exploring alternatives, it joined the small steering committee to organize the spring conference. Miller called the conference at the request of the Women's Advisory Committee to the Secretary of Labor on Women and Defense. Another war emergency, the Korean War, stimulated equal pay policymaking. Steering committee members hoped to use the conference to further two goals: educate the public about equal pay and convince government officials of the need for women in defense work.[114]

Womanpower planning for the Korean War renewed a public focus on working women and gave Frieda Miller another opportunity to fulfill the wish she expressed at the *New York Times* conference in 1943 that women not be denied training because of their sex. In a fourteen-page document, "Employment of Women in an Emergency Period," the Women's Bureau set out proposals to increase the number of women in the labor force. The report not only stressed the need for training in all occupations, including in positions not traditionally held by women, but also made a plea to train women for supervisory positions. This attempt at moral persuasion for equity in the wartime economy accompanied labor forecasting reminding the public that the majority of women already at work were older married, widowed, or divorced women with children to support.[115]

To take advantage of renewed interest in equal pay, the Equal Pay Conference, with urging from Frieda Miller, formed another umbrella organization to keep the policy coalition together. Accordingly, the National Status of Women Committee transformed into the National Committee for Equal Pay. Unlike its two previous incarnations, which focused on mobilizing against the Equal Rights Amendment, this new committee organized around the more specific purpose of promoting federal and state equal pay legislation. Both the AAUW and BPW, with long-standing commitments to equal pay policies, assumed leadership roles in the group.[116]

Sarah Hughes and other BPW leaders attributed stalled action on the ERA to, ironically, the National Woman's Party's aggressive tactics. BPW political strategists believed that constant pressure on members of Congress by NWP activists alienated potential supporters. According to Temple, "Mr. Celler, because he is chairman of the committee, has been particularly exposed to it, and he has taken some rough treatment. I feel sorry for the man. It is not BPW tactics."[117]

Hughes and Marguerite Rawalt hoped to join with the General Federation of Women's Clubs to take leadership of the ERA campaign away from the NWP and renew a campaign characterized by more temperate tactics.[118]

Even though postwar feminist activism failed to generate national policies, evinced by an inability to pass federal equal pay legislation, the ERA, and a status of women bill, state-based activism flourished. Twelve states had equal pay laws by 1952; only two states had such laws in 1940.[119] Twenty-two states had equal pay laws before the passage of the federal Equal Pay Act of 1963.[120] In addition to equal pay laws, thirty-two states ended gender-based restrictions on jury selection and twenty-six states passed minimum wage laws covering women working in intrastate commerce.[121] Sociologist Paul Burstein has argued that Congress did not move on controversial equal pay legislation until state actions demonstrated the existence of favorable public attitudes.[122] State equal rights laws, an important precondition for the passage of federal legislation in 1963, indicate continuity between postwar activism and modern feminism.

The coalition to promote the women's economic agenda remained in place throughout the 1950s, although the contentious deliberations of the National Committee for Equal Pay revealed a split among the policy partners over issues such as the ERA and the role of the Women's Bureau in equal pay enforcement. Republican Alice Leopold, Dwight D. Eisenhower's replacement for Democrat Frieda Miller, favored the BPW's point of view and alienated longstanding allies from labor unions, the National Council of Jewish Women, the League of Women Voters, the National Council of Catholic Women, and the National Council of Negro Women. Still, as the next chapter shows, community-based employment placement programs maintained the link between the government and the grassroots.

CHAPTER 2

Creating Earning Opportunities

The Womanpower Focus
of Alice Leopold, 1953-1961

"COMMUNITY BOOSTERS in Bootstrap Booms," an essay in the August 5, 1957, issue of *Life*, reported that U.S. towns, cities, and states searching for economic prosperity chartered publicly owned and financed development corporations to attract new businesses. Greeneville, Tennessee, lured a new Magnavox television plant to the area; a picture of the plant shows rows and rows of women working in electronics. Ironically Greeneville, a tobacco town prior to World War II, aggressively courted new business enterprise to ensure that returning GIs would remain in town. By the 1950s women, not men, powered the consumer economy.[1]

When President Dwight D. Eisenhower appointed Alice Leopold Women's Bureau director in 1953, a burgeoning consumer economy creating job vacancies and a need for two paychecks per family tempered the postwar backlash against working women Frieda Miller had to combat. Alice Kessler-Harris explains that beginning in the 1950s the proportion of women in the labor force "crept upward" from 39 percent of the labor force in 1950 to 35 percent in 1965.[2] A scarcity of consumer goods during World War II caused well-paid war workers to put an unprecedented 29.6 billion dollars in savings. The postwar spending spree spurred record economic growth that the small Depression-era generation of young workers could not sustain. Acute shortages in traditionally female-dominated occupations, such as clerical work and teaching, toppled prejudices against married women working and eased discrimination against older women. More and more retail stores and offices welcomed women from minority groups. Women from the suburbs worked to help their families maintain a standard of living dictated by the consumer culture. Home mortgages, cars, and the educational needs of three or four children required two incomes. Even though most of these women waited until their children reached school age to enter the labor market, an increasing number of women with young children at home sought paid employment; the number of working women with children under six at home increased by a quarter.[3] By 1960 the typical new entrant to the labor market was a married, middle-aged woman with children. According to William O'Neill, working women "radically altered" the workforce "without anyone noticing it."[4]

O'Neill's statement might be true of the American public, but Rosalind Rosenberg argues that the government "rediscovered womanpower" during this period.[5] Indeed, the Labor Department, increasingly committed to ending shortages in skilled occupations, encouraged women to make permanent commitments to work. Womanpower goals strengthened the Women's Bureau's ties with professional women's organizations and diminished further the reform coalition for protective labor legislation.

Paradoxically, this revision of women's place in the labor force did not lead to aggressive advocacy for equal rights legislation by either the Women's Bureau or women's organizations, as fifties conservatism stalled feminist activism inside and outside the federal government. Departmental restructuring and the anti-ideology, anti-special interest bias of the Eisenhower administration ended the bureau's legislative program. Instead, consistent with the antiregulatory orientation of the Republican Party, the bureau championed the power of individual initiative to create "bootstrap booms" in the labor market. A reorganization plan authorized by Labor Secretary James P. Mitchell integrating women's programming throughout the Labor Department further undermined political goals, although the plan did not work well in practice because bureaus and divisions stubbornly refused to expend resources to evaluate women's economic contributions. The Women's Bureau's marginality paralleled the declining political power of women's organizations: "Men dominated political and intellectual life, and women suffered the erosion of the separate spheres that had provided a significant power base for them at the turn of the century, without being compensated by the genuine sexual integration of major institutions."[6] Organized feminism failed to prevent the dissolution of women's divisions within the Democratic and Republican political parties. Several women's organizations retreated into public service projects. In this bureaucratic and political climate, Alice Leopold abandoned legislative advocacy in favor of a commitment to career and job placement as the sole solution to women's economic and social problems without engendering too much resistance from women's organizations.

Consequently, the Women's Bureau's public service orientation failed to address conflicts women experienced between the burdens of fifties pronatalism and economic responsibilities. Experts urged women to avoid "momism"—suffocating behavior that prevented children from acting independently—but at the same time to be ever present. Popular pediatrician Benjamin Spock warned against working mothers who pursued their own needs at the expense of their children's. He declared confidently that children of working mothers felt abandoned and were more likely to become juvenile delinquents as a result.[7] Leopold spoke out against experts' prognostications that working women caused juvenile delinquency, but ideological battles were not at the forefront of the bureau's program even though social expectations that women's primary responsibility lie with home and family advanced discriminatory practices that kept women out of the very jobs the Women's Bureau began to promote. Kessler-Harris describes the power of ideology this way: "A carefully regulated labor market rooted in conceptions of women as homebound had consistently denied women access to jobs with responsibility, decent pay, promotion, and policy-making power."[8] Throughout this period, women worked, but 80 percent of them labored in jobs typed as female, nonunionized service jobs with poor pay and few benefits.[9] Nonetheless, advocating that the state regulate employment practices did not jibe with President Eisenhower's vision of the benefits of voluntary, cooperative policies.

Robert Griffith explains that an ideology of "the corporate commonwealth"—a vision of "a harmonious corporate society without class conflict, unbridled acquisitiveness, and contentious party politics"—informed Eisenhower's approach to governing.[10] In reaction to what he perceived as New Deal and Fair Deal statism favoring organized labor, which led to class conflict, Eisenhower advocated federal activities that persuaded business and labor to voluntarily set aside particularistic agendas to effect a national consensus on the economy. Through the use of public relations techniques in particular, executive departments sought voluntary policy alliances among business, labor, state and local agencies, and organizations much in the same way Greeneville's community leaders did in negotiating with Magnavox. In addition to a presidential committee on public relations, departments initiated publicity campaigns and formed policymaking advisory committees to replace regulation and enforcement.[11]

Democrats Maurice Tobin and Frieda Miller offered their resignations to the first Republican president in the welfare state, who appointed Martin Durkin, president of the AFL-affiliated United Association of Journeymen and Apprentices of the Plumbing and Pipe Fitting Industry, and Republican secretary of state for Connecticut, Alice Leopold, to replace them. Durkin supported Eisenhower but attempted to put through a labor agenda of his own, including minimum wage regulation in government contracts, revision of the Taft-Hartley Act, and the appointment of a CIO leader as assistant secretary. The Eisenhower administration would not support any of these goals, and the "plumber" in a cabinet of millionaires resigned in frustration after eight months on the job to be replaced by James P. Mitchell.[12] Durkin's brief, troubled tenure presaged an uncertain future for the Labor Department's welfare state policies in a Republican administration.

In Mitchell and Leopold, Eisenhower found labor officials less keen on regulating business enterprise and more willing to adjust public policies to fit the cooperative intent of the "corporate commonwealth." Both appointees had professional experience as personnel managers for large department store chains; and as industrial relations experts representing employers, their labor-management experience favored the tools of mediation and persuasion. Mitchell's perspective on labor relations, from personnel work and a stint as a manpower planner in the federal government during World War II, gave him enough credibility to become one of the president's advisers on economic policy, a position of influence previous labor secretaries had failed to attain.[13] Leopold, too, benefited from insider status, becoming assistant to the secretary of labor for women's affairs in 1954.

Alice Leopold became the first director in the Women's Bureau's history to come from party politics. Mary Anderson and Frieda Miller, who came from the ranks of Progressive Era labor and reform organizations, not from political parties, avoided partisan politics. With a reputation as a committed Progressive Era social reformer, Anderson seemed above politics; she served in both Republican and Democratic administrations. Labor economist Frieda Miller came to the federal government from a state labor department. It is likely that male politicians in the Democratic Party did not take Miller seriously enough to tap her as a party functionary.[14] The *New York Times* reported that another state labor official, Republican Mary Rice Marrow, would probably replace Frieda Miller. Only party affiliation distinguished Marrow's resume from Miller's; a former industrial secretary for the YWCA and settlement house worker, Marrow headed the Pennsylvania Department of Women and Children, Hours, and Minimum Wages.[15] Alice Leopold got the post instead. A party stalwart through and through, Leopold began her political career with leadership positions in the Connecticut League of Women Voters and then pursued state office holding; she eventually became a Republican member of the general assembly, secretary of state, and the first woman in the state to serve as acting governor.[16]

Unlike Marrow, Leopold had policymaking experience on the national level as one of the few female advisers to Eisenhower's presidential campaign in 1952 and as a member of the Inter-Governmental Relations Commission charged to make recommendations where federal aid duplicated local programs or undermined state sovereignty. Critics of the commission accused the president of "reevaluating federalism" and proposing a "counterrevolution of the welfare state concept of the New Deal and Fair Deal."[17] Leopold continued to serve on the commission after her confirmation to the labor post.

Leopold's position in the Labor Department did not prevent her from going out on the hustings to clarify where the Democrats and Republicans parted company on the role of the state in the economy, as is evident in one of her many speeches promoting the Republican Party: "This is a Republican administration in which employment figures have not only set an all-time record high . . . for the Democrats have never and cannot now possibly conceive such high employment without a dole."[18] Her zeal in representing the Republican administration took her to the heights of hyperbole in a speech to the Camden, New Jersey, Republican Women's Club: "I am speaking of the greatest leadership our country has known since another dedicated general—Washington—laid down his arms to help shape a new nation. There is today the same dedication, the same love of country, the same accord with all the people."[19]

Much of Leopold's rhetoric implied that prestigious and lucrative positions became available to those women who applied themselves. Sex differences had psychological roots instead of institutional ones. Women possessed less ambition and competitive zeal than men, characteristics that made them less effective in the workplace; they inevitably lost in competition with men because they chose to let family responsibilities circumscribe their tenure as workers. Thus, personal choices determined women's differing experiences in the labor market. Leopold took care not to propose that women give up their roles as wives and mothers, but she argued that such a choice came at an inevitable economic cost.[20]

To Leopold, though, the "double burden" no longer constituted a woman's lot in life because a division of labor by sex ended during World War II when women had the opportunity to prove themselves as skilled, competent workers. The household, no longer the sole preserve of the woman, became a shared responsibility between husband and wife—a domestic "corporate commonwealth." Borrowing Virginia Woolf's anthem that each woman needed an independent income and a room of her own, Leopold declared that women no longer required a separate room because they could share economic, political, and social power with men: "Only through such sharing can we learn to live and work together, as men and women in a society in which we all work *for* instead of *against* each other, all for 'the common good' [Leopold's emphasis]."[21] In a speech at a national convention of the American Federation of Soroptimists, Leopold chastised women for not seeking positions in business and politics. Additionally, she bemoaned the fact that the majority of women "are still in the traditional fields of teaching, nursing, the social sciences, and kindred fields," even though "changing patterns of our civilization have permitted more women to enter technical fields."[22]

The Eisenhower administration purged other female bureaucrats sympathetic to the New Deal. Jane Hoey, one of the architects of the Social Security Act, and Anna Rosenberg, secretary of defense in the Truman administration, joined Frieda Miller in the private sector. Eleanor Roosevelt, the most famous casualty of the transfer of power from the Democrats to Republicans, lost her job as UN ambassador to Republican Pauline Lord. Oveta Culp Hobby, secretary of Health, Education, and Welfare and Eisenhower's token female cabinet officer, actively limited the role of the agency in promoting and administrating social reforms.

Agencies in the Eisenhower administration focused on building cooperative partnerships with business. Thus, the Labor Department became a "national clearinghouse" of statistical information on the nation's workforce to be used by states, local communities, and businesses.[23] The Bureaus of Labor Standards and Labor Statistics assisted private enterprise by compiling information about the workforce, and conversely, publicized industries' employment requirements to the public. Beginning in 1954, per a directive from Eisenhower, the Departments of Labor and Commerce published monthly joint figures on employment and unemployment to enable businesses to plan effectively.[24]

The Republican administration did not repudiate social welfare entitlements constructed by Democratic administrations, however. Social Security, minimum wage, and unemployment insurance entitlements remained part of the federal apparatus, but Eisenhower assumed that maintenance of existing entitlements precluded the creation of new programs.[25] Preferring voluntary compliance with existing welfare state regulations, Secretary Mitchell initiated educational campaigns to sell employers on the utility of existing social welfare measures to economic growth. His intention was clear in his annual report for 1954 which stated that unemployment insurance "helped maintain markets for business through its contribution to the purchasing power in the local community, the state, and the Nation" and aided business by allowing skilled workers to remain available if they were a casualty of seasonal layoffs or retooling.[26]

Extending coverage and benefits of existing entitlements and support of collective bargaining remained part of the Labor Department's mission, but aggressive promotion of additional federal legislation had all but ceased to occur. Although the secretary's annual reports touted the department's efforts on behalf of increasing employees' benefits, overall plans for bureaus and divisions carried out Eisenhower's philosophy that enforcement belonged within the purview of the states and that the federal role in the economy should remain in the realm of moral persuasion to achieve coveted policies. This meant that each bureau and division concentrated on compiling facts about employment, unemployment, and working conditions as a service to state labor departments, federal advisory committees, and business groups. Faith that facts would induce cooperation between interest groups resulted in the proliferation of advisory committees and planning conferences. According to Mitchell, by bringing representatives from industry, government, education, and labor together in Washington, a message of cooperation would trickle down to their constituencies: "The Department, therefore, must depend on multipliers—those who, purely on a voluntary basis, work for the good of a cause and get others to help."[27]

A damaged relationship with business caused by flak over a 1947 informational leaflet, "Women's Stake in Unions," haunted the Women's Bureau in the Eisenhower administration. Business representatives, pointing to arguments in the leaflet that unions helped women by "giving them a voice in collective bargaining, better jobs, higher pay, shorter hours, and seniority rights," and that women's organizations should "understand" union programs, charged that the federal government aggressively promoted unionization to female workers.[28] Aware of the potential problems the pamphlet might cause in the pro-business administration, lobbyists from several women's organizations met with Bertha Adkins, assistant to the chairman of the Republican National Committee, to make a case for retaining the Women's Bureau even before Dwight and Mamie Eisenhower unpacked at the White House.

Adkins invited the group to outline the Women's Bureau's program and to justify why such a program should be expanded. The subsequent report included plans for a president's commission on the status of women, which would require additional funding for administration. The proposed commission would develop policies aimed at placement of women in training programs and in higher education, study the labor market to evaluate the persistence of discrimination, and find ways to improve the civil and political status of women.[29]

Leopold did not feel beholden to traditional allies, because she believed that a taxpayer-supported public bureaucracy charged to serve all working women should not promote a divisive political program. Her antipathy to economic regulation and interest group politics became obvious to the public in dramatic fashion when she used her first press conference as Women's Bureau director to suspend active opposition to the Equal Rights Amendment. The press conference put out the welcome mat to groups not traditionally part of the policy alliance, including the National Woman's Party and the National Association of Manufacturers. In order to facilitate a broad-based coalition to plan for the efficient utilization of female workers, Leopold announced a conference "to consider program objectives and legislation of mutual interest to the Department of Labor and national women's organizations, civic organizations, and other groups."[30] Evaluation of "program objectives and legislation" included a review of the Women's Bureau's historic opposition to the ERA. Until then, no action would be forthcoming. The National Woman's Party interpreted Leopold's professed "no position" on the ERA as the equivalent of endorsing the amendment, which they publicized in the October and November 1954 issues of their magazine *Equal Rights*.[31] A month after the NWP's publicity, the CIO passed a resolution during its Sixteenth Constitutional Convention criticizing the Women's Bureau's flip-flop on the ERA.[32]

Secretary Mitchell acquiesced to labor union demands and clarified the department's position in 1955, albeit weakly, by testifying on Senate Joint Resolution 49, the Equal Rights Amendment, that he "could not recommend favorable action on the Amendment."[33] At Leopold's request in 1954, the department's solicitor reevaluated the Equal Rights Amendment, Senate Joint Resolution 111, and ruled that the proposed joint resolution did not necessarily endanger existing protective labor laws, which offered a rationale for at least a neutral position.[34] Secretary Mitchell conveyed this opinion to the Senate Judiciary Committee. When a second joint resolution appeared in 1955, Leopold urged the secretary to stand pat on the solicitor's 1954 ruling, but the secretary changed his mind and testified in opposition to the amendment.[35] The reasons why Secretary Mitchell ignored Leopold's desire to maintain a neutral position on this divisive issue are murky. However, in opposing the ERA, Mitchell threw a political bone to labor unions increasingly critical of his department. The Women's Bureau had to defer to the Department of Labor, but Leopold tried to assuage equal rights feminists with public statements deferring active opposition to the ERA.[36]

Leopold's actions in part reflected the weakening of the once formidable anti–Equal Rights Amendment coalition. Susan Levine, historian of the AAUW, believes that, for women in the 1950s, the ERA was a "minor issue."[37] The AAUW, like the Women's Bureau, took no action on the amendment during this period. A proposal to overturn the AAUW's long-standing opposition to the amendment lost by a narrow margin during its annual national convention in 1952 resulting in a neutral position that lasted throughout the decade. One of the most vociferous and active opponents of the amendment, the Women's Trade Union League, disbanded in 1950. The declining political influence and class-based politics of the union movement contributed to the end of the WTUL. Moreover, women in unions began to question the purpose of protective labor legislation. Representatives from the UAW attending the National Manpower Council's meetings on womanpower opposed protective labor legislation because state laws defining women as a separate class of worker enabled employers to justify discriminatory practices.[38] However, as Nancy Gabin argues, feminists within the labor movement, lacking the support of a women's movement, could not change the AFL and CIO's traditional opposition to the amendment.[39] Even the venerable Eleanor Roosevelt changed her position on the ERA in 1953 from opposition to support.[40]

The absence of active opposition to the ERA was more a product of political malaise than realignments among women's organizations. Several organizations in the Women's Bureau coalition retreated from interest group politics and embraced more utilitarian projects. Anticommunist hysteria caused some organizations to moderate ideological rhetoric for fear of creating any hint of political radicalism. Rochelle Gatlin suggests that "feminism, like communism, was demoted to the status of a simple minded, outmoded and dangerous ideology."[41] Moreover, service-oriented goals fit the sensibilities of middle-class suburban housewives who began to dominate the memberships of prominent women's organizations, such as the AAUW and the LWV. Suburban voluntarism emerged from what William Whyte called a "social ethic," described by William O'Neill as "a value system embracing adaptability, cooperation, mutual aid, respect for others and community involvement."[42] Women's organizations followed the "social ethic" at the expense of promoting an ideology that women had special needs and concerns as a group.

The American Association of University Women provides a case
in point. The composition of the AAUW changed during this period:
"Two-thirds of the membership was under forty-six years of age and
half were mothers. Forty-one percent of the membership identified
themselves as housewives."[43] Demographic and geographical changes
swelled state and local branch membership. Branches dominated by
proponents of the "social ethic" clashed with older, professional
women who served as national officers. Leaders of the Status of
Women Committee in particular wanted to press on with a quintessential feminist agenda. Sociologist Rosamonde Boyd chaired the
committee in 1952 and sought a reevaluation of the ERA and protection legislation. Her successor, unapologetic feminist Gertrude Fariss,
also resisted a movement within the organization to focus on narrow,
service-oriented goals. Fariss, a professional educator who became
active in the AAUW in the 1930s, fought to maintain a national commitment to public activism. Levine quotes her as saying, "I have
never once mentioned finance folders, money management portfo-
lios, or civil defense."[44]

The tension between the two camps manifested in a plan to
merge the Status of Women Committee with the Legislation Committee. Pro-merger forces failed to disband the Status of Women
Committee during the 1957 national convention, but the fight
weakened the cause for women's rights advocacy within the organization. New members favored equity rather than equal rights advocacy to such an extent that the creation of a nonpartisan roster of
qualified women for government posts became the most important
achievement of the status of women program during the 1950s.[45]
Apparently, the AAUW shared the Women's Bureau's faith in
"bootstrap booms."

The YWCA experienced a similar ideological cleansing, as new
members reevaluated the efficacy of a separate women's program.
YWCA historian Susan Lynn suggests that the membership adapted
a centrist point of view on women's status. Most members did not
endorse the most conservative ideology of the period that dictated
women's activity be confined to home and hearth, nor did they
accept feminist assumptions that women could combine career and
family. The centrist view, consistent with the values of the "social
ethic," prevailed: "What was notably missing from the debate
within the YWCA about women's roles was any forthright challenge

to the prevalent belief that women should assume primary responsibility for the care of children and the home. Rather, the position taken most frequently was that women should combine the responsibilities of family care with those of work or volunteer activities."[46] The retirement of feminist group consciousness resulted in a plan to merge the YWCA and the YMCA and the prevalence of "family life" programs appealing to homemakers. The National Board opposed the merger in 1954, as professionals in the national office sought to maintain a feminist sensibility within the organization.

The League of Women Voters' nonpartisan, community service mission contributed to membership growth in the fifties. Members preferred to participate in study groups, voter service, and local political issues. Susan Ware states that only 4 percent expected the league to support legislation.[47] Between 1950 and 1958 membership grew by 44 percent, with 1,050 local branches active in forty-eight states. These women subscribed to the organizational mania characteristic of suburban communities—more than one-third of the membership belonged to five or more organizations. Eugenia Kaledin argues that membership in the LWV "offered an outlet for the energies of educated women all over the country who wanted to inject a dimension of humanitarian concern into active public life."[48]

Perhaps understanding the shifting goals of prominent women's organizations, Secretary Mitchell attempted to convince representatives attending a conference in 1954 that women might be better served by the entire Department of Labor rather than by a bureau bent on limiting their opportunities by advocating protective labor legislation.[49] Alice Leopold did not enter the debate between women's groups and the Labor Department. Traditional Women's Bureau allies, led by Margaret Mealy of the National Council of Catholic Women and the National Council of Jewish Women's lobbyist, Olya Margolin, did not accept Mitchell's logic and drafted a lengthy response arguing that the progress women had made in economic, social, and political life "has blinded some to the tremendous obstacles that have impeded even this progress, and which continue to account for the special nature of the problems that still confront women."[50] This response indicates that feminist activism remained alive at least among the professional lobbyists representing national women's organizations.

Despite special pleading for a separate women's agency, including a request from women's organizations to meet with the committee formed to reorganize the Department of Labor, outside reviewers recommended abolishing the Women's Bureau. To make departmental work more efficient and cost effective, Secretary Mitchell invited "impartial, knowledgeable, and sympathetic private citizens" to review all of the programs within the department.[51] The "impartial" panel included three academics—J. Douglas Brown, a dean at Princeton University, Eli Ginsberg from Columbia University, and Chancellor Clark Kerr of the University of California; an industrial relations expert, Cyrus S. Ching; and William T. Stead, vice president of the Federal Reserve Board. Organized labor did not contribute to the review. The original reorganization plan, submitted by the secretary to the Bureau of the Budget, abolished the Women's Bureau and transferred its functions and personnel to other areas, created a "super grade" for the director with the title of assistant secretary of labor for women's affairs, and abolished the offices of director and assistant director.[52] President Eisenhower's message to Congress on the Reorganization Plan of 1954 supported the plan to abolish the Women's Bureau because women were "represented in all of the 466 occupations listed by the Bureau of the Census and their total number in the labor force approached 19 million."[53] He added that labor standards covering women as well as men eliminated the need for policies for women as a separate interest group.

In the end, the secretary used his administrative discretion to keep the Women's Bureau intact, but Leopold also monitored all projects related to women as assistant to the labor secretary for women's affairs, not as assistant secretary of labor for women's affairs. It is very likely that Mitchell chose the status quo over elevating Leopold to assistant secretary of labor. Even so, in making Leopold intradepartmental coordinator for women, the Reorganization Plan increased her power and authority but compromised the Women's Bureau's function and future as an autonomous division because it cut out territory that justified increased responsibilities, appropriations, and staff over time. The Bureau of Labor Statistics assumed responsibility for collecting statistics on women's employment from the Census Bureau, and the Bureau of Labor Standards coordinated all departmental activities relating to labor standards legislation.[54]

Instead of benefiting from programmatic adjustments focusing on women workers, the Women's Bureau emerged from the women's affairs scheme more dependent on other bureaus and divisions for research data, public relations assistance, and legal research. The task fell to Leopold to represent the Department of Labor's women's program to government agencies and to collaborate with internal bureaus and division chiefs to determine the research, statistical analysis, and publications needed to execute womanpower goals. At least the assistant director position remained in place to manage the day-today activities of the Women's Bureau, while Leopold organized departmentwide projects.[55]

Winifred Helmes, a member of the AAUW's executive staff from 1951 to 1954, became assistant director. Helmes, a former history professor at the University of Minnesota and Louisiana State University and author of a biography of Minnesota governor John A. Johnson, became the third historian hired since World War II.[56] Just months before accepting the assistant director appointment, Helmes, as the status of women associate with the AAUW, worked on a joint survey of part-time employment with the Women's Bureau.[57] Her appointment reinforced ties with the AAUW.

The attempt to integrate women's interests throughout the Labor Department failed, however. Divisions' and bureaus' persistent reluctance to incorporate employment data on women inspired another memo war between Women's Bureau staffers and their colleagues in the department. Two years after reorganization, statistician Mildred Barber, particularly disturbed by the continuing failure of the Bureau of Labor Statistics to consider women workers, turned to her typewriter. In an extensive memo to a colleague in the BLS, Anna Behrens, Barber pointed to "gaps in our research and statistical program," including lack of data on female workers by industry, a dearth of cost-of-living information for single employed women, and "little collection of data by sex for industries other than manufacturing."[58] Further, she complained that the Women's Bureau did not have the professional staff to analyze statistical data collected by other agencies.

Women's Bureau staff member Jean A. Wells met with Harold Goldstein of the BLS to raise concerns about employment projections data. Initially, Goldstein rejected a proposal to create separate figures for men and women, but he later agreed to allow a Women's

Bureau employee familiar with women's employment patterns to analyze the data for possible adjustments in the number of women in certain occupations.[59] Other bureaus and divisions did not want to assign staff members to analyze data by sex; but, according to Barber, the Women's Bureau did not have the staff to undertake the task independently.

In keeping with the customer service approach in the Labor Department, the bureau's Civil and Political Status Division remained intact, but only to provide legal advice to constituencies upon request, because drafting and advocating agency bills ceased to be a function.[60] Agency bills, which had represented organized labor and the Labor Department's interest in using the power of the state to require recalcitrant businesses to adopt fair labor practices, had no place in an administration functioning on the axiom that positive government-business relations were an essential precondition for a healthy economy. As a result, Leopold took no action on leftover agency bills promoted by Frieda Miller that were reintroduced in Congress between 1954 and 1956, including the Legal Status of Women bill.[61] In addition, support to women's organizations seeking legislative change suffered under the new regime. Margaret Mealy of the National Council of Catholic Women and a member of the National Committee for Equal Pay expressed her exasperation with the women's affairs program to Secretary Mitchell: "Each year as we have looked toward hearings [on federal equal pay legislation], we have come face to face with the problem of supporting data . . . may we respectfully request that you include the securing of data in the field of unequal pay."[62]

Nevertheless, the Labor Department could not avoid taking a position on federal equal pay for equal work legislation. A broad coalition of women's organizations, including the formidable pro-business Business and Professional Women's Clubs, with 156,000 members in 1956, worked for years to pass a draft federal equal pay bill with enforcement provisions modeled on the National Labor Relations Act. On the other hand, business groups campaigned against the equal pay bills introduced in Congress in 1948 and 1950 that put teeth into compliance by allowing for federal court prosecution and imposition of criminal penalties for violations.[63] When Edith Green, Democratic representative from Oregon, reintroduced equal pay bills with similar enforcement authority in 1954 and 1955, business groups again began to mobilize in opposition. Leopold sided with Secretary Mitchell in supporting a Republican bill with weaker enforcement provisions to counteract Green's action.

The department instead endorsed H.R. 7172, introduced by Representative Frances Bolton, a Republican from Ohio, as a compromise measure. The Bolton bill, based on the results of a questionnaire on equal pay legislation sent to one thousand leaders from labor, business, finance, education, and women's organizations, was an approach to policy formation consistent with the goals of the "corporate commonwealth." It amended the Fair Labor Standards Act (FLSA) to make unlawful the payment of unequal wage rates to women doing comparable work and prohibited an employer from dismissing or discriminating against an employee who filed suit under the law. In amending the FLSA, the bill placed the burden on the employee to file suit rather than providing the federal government with investigatory powers, allowed the court to assess damages based on either a "show of good faith or a willful violation," an approach long championed by the National Association of Manufacturers, and vested administration in the independent Wage, Hour, and Public Contracts Division.[64] Leopold supported the Bolton bill yet suggested to solicitor Stuart Rothman that the legislation be revised to codify a broader administrative role for the Labor Department: "To place authority in the Secretary of Labor would enable him to integrate major policy aspects of equal pay enforcement with general Department programs affecting women's status."[65] Even Republican bureaucrats found that the promise of expanded enforcement authority proved too tempting to pass up. Secretary Mitchell accepted Leopold's argument and conveyed her suggestions to Representative Bolton.[66] As a result, the version introduced on January 14, 1954, included a provision empowering the Labor Department to set standards to determine which jobs involved "work of comparable character or skills."[67] The Bolton bill died in committee, but Republican labor officials tried to revive interest in compromise legislation similar to Bolton's among women's organizations.

The Labor Department promoted another equal pay bill in 1956 to amend the FLSA because Eisenhower mentioned support for equal pay in his State of the Union message. Since several equal pay bills were introduced in the Eighty-fourth Congress, including another Bolton bill, the Labor Department's action frustrated women's organizations. They failed to convince Leopold to drop the administration measure. Activists believed that equal pay legislation had become the stuff of partisan politics and that the sheer number of competing bills would give the chairman of the House Labor Committee a reason to delay action yet again.[68] Internal squabbles occurred as well. Civil and Political Status Division chief Alice Morrison complained to Helmes that she lacked the necessary data on men's and women's wages to support a case for any equal pay for equal work measure.[69]

Frances Bolton introduced another, even more watered-down equal pay bill in 1959 after several bills failed to pass between 1954 and 1957. This new version simply directed the Secretary of Labor to study wage differentials between men and women, to "make known the psychological effect of the discrimination that now exists," and to publicize the successful outcome of state equal pay legislation.[70] Bolton took a different tack because she did not think members of Congress would support a bill with enforcement provisions without compelling evidence of widespread discrimination. Moreover, she did not want to ask the Secretary of Labor to engage in an extensive study of wage rates without authorizing legislation.[71] Even though members of the National Committee for Equal Pay (NCEP) wanted to stand by a champion for equal pay in Congress, they could not endorse legislation without enforcement mechanisms. Affiliated women's organizations agreed that such legislation would be "a backward step" that would impede progress to get regulatory language into law.[72] They had no inclination to support further study of whether or not wage differentials actually existed. There can be no doubt that disagreements over enforcement provisions contributed to lack of congressional action on equal pay legislation until 1963.

Business groups also challenged state minimum wage laws, especially provisions that established wage boards to determine minimum wages for particular industries. Employers in several states attacked these wage boards because they often included representatives from organized labor. When representatives from the District of Columbia retail trade industry complained to the Department of Labor that Alice Morrison testified in favor of a retail trade wage board, Administrative Operations Division chief

Stella Manor offered to clear all comments germane to wage boards with the secretary's office.[73] As a result, Morrison kept a low profile at a subsequent conference on a New Jersey minimum wage bill aimed at female-employing industries, reporting to Leopold, "My function, of course, was to explain the various alternatives and illustrate them in terms of state experience without expressing preferences."[74]

Head of the Civil and Political Status Division, the lawyer Alice Morrison, hired by Mary Anderson in 1941, found program integration and subsequent neglect of legislative goals intolerable. With the exception of a brief stint in private law practice in Duluth, Minnesota, Morrison's entire professional career involved employment regulation. She enforced minimum wage and maximum hours laws for the North Dakota Department of Labor, then accepted various positions in the federal government researching the earnings and hours of women.[75] The veteran bureaucrat attempted to retain legislative work in spite of programmatic adjustments favoring employment placement. Few staffers escaped a Morrison memo criticizing the abandonment of legislative goals. Complaining that the Women's Bureau's request for statistical support from the Bureau of Labor Statistics did not include equal pay data, Morrison urged Helmes to make sure that data be made available on "wage rates paid for comparable work of men and women by the same employer in the same plant and by industry and occupation."[76] In a memo to colleague Miriam Keeler, Morrison charged that the annual report for 1956 underestimated legislative programs, and she suggested that the division go back to a previous practice of writing separate reports on each legislative initiative, such as minimum wage, equal pay, and legal status.[77] To Frances Ambursen, Morrison expressed alarm that twenty-five remaining copies of the bulletin on laws regulating weight lifting were put on reserve in the department's publication room with no plans to reissue the bulletin for public consumption.[78]

Leopold preferred to spend resources on particular employment areas rather than attend to ties with interest groups deemed by the Republicans unable to envision cooperation, especially organized labor. No activity better illustrates the difference between Miller and Leopold than the fate of the Trade Union Advisory Committee. The advisory committee of labor union women, so important to policymaking from 1945 to 1953, became the Women's Advisory Committee under Leopold's directive that its membership be expanded to include representatives from business, women's organizations, and those unions "with a large female membership."[79] By 1957, interest group advisory committees disappeared altogether so that bigger delegations could have access to policymaking via conferences called on special topics.[80]

The practice of building cooperative arrangements with a varied crowd of advisers with interests far afield from the Women's Bureau coalition began early in Leopold's tenure. Guided by the Department of Labor's preference for broader coalitions, the 1955 conference, "The Effective Use of Womanpower," drew six hundred delegates including representatives from professional, vocational, and trade organizations. Leopold and Helmes considered the title "Patterns of Partnership" for the 1955 conference, which announced a direction denying women interest group status: "We want to avoid the old battle of the sexes idea and pitch a conference around the idea of men and women working together and maintaining the Nation's economy."[81] In fact, Undersecretary of Labor Arthur Larson believed that the classification of workers into special groups was communistic.[82]

Despite Leopold's rhetoric stressing cooperation, the conference did not encourage participatory policy formation characteristic of the previous reconversion conferences organized by Frieda Miller. Instead, experts on women's workforce participation, primarily academics and industrial relations professionals, presented analyses on employment opportunities. This reliance on experts reflected the individualistic nature of feminism during this period. Women writers and academics more so than women's organizations challenged the ideology of domesticity so prevalent during the 1950s. The Women's Bureau gave feminist academics, Barnard sociologist Mirra Komarovsky and Harvard anthropologist Frances Kluckhorn, platforms for advocating women's importance to public life. Panels on "The Woman Who Works," "New Horizons for Women," and "Shortage Occupations" put forward a positive outlook on women's economic future. Thus, the conference format provided the Department of Labor with an opportunity to downplay the argument that women's weaker position in the economy required state intervention. Komarovsky urged conference participants to transcend the barriers of the sex-segregated labor market: "May I remind you that women constitute 90 percent of librarians, 60 percent of all welfare workers, and 80 percent of teachers? I believe that many a first-rate male teacher is lost to teaching because it is a feminine and underpaid occupation, and many a woman scientist would be more competent than the man who takes her place in the laboratory because it is not a feminine field."[83]

The conference did not avoid controversy entirely. Several male panelists from business and academia used the public forum to criticize working women. Psychiatrist Leo H. Bartemeier, a panelist on the topic "Horizons for Women," explained that women with young children worked out of a sense of neurotic competition with other women for material possessions. He warned that these competitive women denied their young children emotional support. Female academics on the panel, Kluckhorn and the New York University psychologist Marie Jahoda, disagreed with Bartemeier, pointing out that the isolation of the homemaker was far more problematic than the working wife and mother.[84] In a lively exchange between panelists considering the topic "The Woman Who Works, as Others See Her, and as She Sees Herself" moderated by Helmes, male executives emphasized female executives' inability to assume positions of authority, whereas career women raised the issue of obstacles to advancement.[85]

For the first time in its history, the Women's Bureau encouraged women to enter the professions and technical occupations that required more commitment to training and education. Although two recessions occurred during the Eisenhower administration, many occupations in technical fields and scientific professions faced shortages. Technological advances created new occupations, a trend that began after World War II. In its second term, the Eisenhower administration established an advisory committee to study ways to foster a more qualified, technologically sophisticated workforce. One of the committee's reports to the president pointed to barriers preventing women from entering scientific fields.[86] The Women's Bureau followed up on this recommendation by publicizing scientific fields for women. Prescriptions that women pursue occupations that welcomed their feminine perspectives or avoid occupations dominated by men became a thing of the past. Publications incorporated an ideological perspective championing individual choice and ignoring social barriers to advancement; women with the right qualifications would be welcome in traditionally male-dominated fields in science, engineering, and accounting because shortages would mitigate gender bias.[87] *Womanpower,* a report issued by the National Manpower Council in 1957, the same year the Russians launched Sputnik, recommended training women in math and science. Passed a year later, the National Defense Education Act of 1958 provided assistance to women seeking to enter scientific fields.

Attention to the professions did not merely reflect ideological adjustments and a changing labor market but became a necessity with departmental restructuring. Stripped of a significant research role, the Women's Bureau extended its activities beyond budget constraints by engaging various professional organizations in collaborative research projects, which yielded data on women in particular occupations without incurring significant out-of-pocket costs. This arrangement did not always work smoothly, though. The *Monthly Labor Review* refused to publish a joint study with the Association of Women Bankers on female bank executives because it was not of interest to industry. Staff member A. Sullivan expressed her frustration at a failure to get cooperation on the bankers' study to Leopold: "Frankly the attitude taken by the Bureau of Labor Statistics is beyond my comprehension. I thought the Department of Labor and the Women's Bureau were trying to promote among other programs opportunities for wage earners in specific fields of work of which banking certainly is one."[88] Nevertheless, a series on the career choices of female college graduates from the classes of 1955, 1956, and 1957, based on data produced from an alliance with the Vocational Association of America, did reach public view.[89] Traditional allies did not always approve of the Women's Bureau's new concern with professional women. The chairman of the Committee on Women and Child Labor and Minimum Wage for the Missouri State Labor Council, D. Jean Younce, of the International Union of Electrical Workers, asked the Labor Council to persuade the secretary of labor to "redirect" the Women's Bureau's policies toward improving the status of semiskilled and unskilled workers.[90]

Integration of research, legislation, and publicity did not preclude the Women's Bureau program expansion altogether, yet budget increases occurred only in Eisenhower's second term when limited government rhetoric ceased to be a political necessity. Leopold used departmental cooperative goals with the private sector to justify reopening field offices and starting up a new publication. The field office enterprise included the addition of four new staff members to carry out joint projects with states and communities to address employment shortages, especially in nursing, but the new workers did not punch time clocks until 1957. At the same time, a modest four-page publication, "Facts on Women Workers," updated policy partners on women's status. Ever mindful of cost-cutting and efficiency, Leopold assured internal budget administrators that the sheet, a trial run, would be issued only "when we felt we have sufficient materials to justify it."[91]

Alice Morrison expressed frustration in a memo to Leopold that the position descriptions for field representatives ignored traditional constituencies' work for state and federal legislation and overemphasized joint programs with community groups: "Two of our major constituents, women's organizations and state labor departments, seem to be omitted entirely. Although some women's organizations would fall within the category 'community groups' most major organizations function at the state and national, as well as the community level."[92] Frances Whitelock disagreed. Her memo to Leopold outlined how the field representatives could strengthen services to management and support business's renewed interest in community projects. By focusing attention on potential employers, the Women's Bureau would more effectively represent female workers "by bringing to management's attention certain facts which heretofore may not have been emphasized sufficiently in management circles, notably women's capabilities to perform jobs of a high level and the continuous widening of their job horizons."[93]

The women hired as regional representatives had the professional experience to carry out Whitelock's action plan rather than Morrison's. All four new hires had backgrounds in personnel and employment placement and transferred to the Women's Bureau from other positions within the federal civil service, a pattern of recruitment characteristic of Frieda Miller as well. Labor economist Sylvia Pallow was a colleague of Margaret Plunkett on the War Production Board during World War II. Vi Morlan, an employment placement specialist, served in the War Manpower agency during the Korean War and then functioned as a personnel officer with the U.S. Navy. Augusta Clawson also worked for the Navy as a management analyst. Phillis Beattie, a labor economist for the regional office of the Bureau of Labor Statistics in San Francisco, made an internal transfer. The only nongovernment employee, consultant Mildred Horne, came from advertising and public relations.[94]

Several ongoing projects helped the Women's Bureau maintain connections with women's organizations even in the midst of program adjustments de-emphasizing interest group politics. The AAUW's part-time employment study, a survey of the availability of part-time work for older women reentering the labor market begun during Frieda Miller's tenure, remained a program activity into the 1950s. The joint part-time study illustrates how a research activity evolved into a permanent institution that maintained a policy network among state labor departments, the federal government, and women's organizations. From an initial survey, the Madison, Wisconsin, AAUW branch established a "Women's Service Exchange" with the help of Wisconsin governor Walter J. Kohler, who gave the group resources from the state vocational school system, including office space and staff. The exchange both publicized part-time opportunities to women and surveyed the needs of the state's employers.[95]

The formation of the President's Committee for the Employment of Older Workers in 1957 generated more programmatic attention to this group within the Labor Department. The department's Manpower Development Office reactivated an interbureau steering committee on older workers composed of representatives of the Bureau of Employment Security, the Bureau of Labor Statistics, the Women's Bureau, and the Office of Public Information.[96] Sometimes the Manpower Development Office was a bit overzealous in pushing the hiring of older workers. Leopold pointed out to the Director of the Bureau of Employment Security, Seymour Wolfbein, that a pamphlet pointing out the pension savings to companies hiring older workers discouraged hiring women. One line read: "If benefits for dependents include maternity care, the package cost may even be less for the older man."[97] The assistant to the secretary for women's affairs objected to a publication that openly contradicted departmental goals to integrate women's concerns in every publication and program.

The departmental and interbureau older workers' program focused on employment placement. The Women's Bureau did recognize age discrimination as one cause for the underemployment and unemployment of reentry women, yet the prescription for change did not involve legislated remedies. The joint private and public employment exchange in Wisconsin, sponsored by the AAUW, served as a prototype for the Earning Opportunities Forum for Mature Women (EOF) established by Alice Leopold in 1957—one-day workshops organized to put women into contact with employers and state and local employment counselors—as its contribution to the older worker initiative. The community-based forums brought employment seekers and employers together on a voluntary, informal basis, which ostensibly would end age discrimination. These events led to activism unrelated to political action. Forum gatherings allowed Leopold and her colleagues to suggest to participating women's organizations the formation of committees to monitor hiring of older women in their communities. One recommended task for the new committees involved contacting every employer placing a want ad for "women under 35" and asking "why he specified a certain age, and what exactly is the drawback to hiring older, qualified women."[98]

Despite the fact that the EOF programs captured the lion's share of the Women's Bureau's resources, Leopold promoted the forums as "community-action" programs initiated by private organizations, a goal she explained in an article for the *National Business Woman,* the publication of the National Federation of Business and Professional Women's Clubs: "The Earning Opportunities Forum is essentially a community program and its effectiveness derives from common interests and joint endeavors."[99] Indeed, the Women's Bureau actively sought sponsorship of the EOFs among women's organizations, culminating in a formal arrangement with the BPW. The national BPW agreed to encourage its local and state career advancement committees to make organizing the EOFs a priority. Service organizations outside of the loop of established policy partners—Altrusa, Pilot, Quota, Soroptimist, and Zonta—worked with the BPW to organize this community-action program.[100] The Women's Bureau leaflet "What a Community Can Do to Train Mature Women for Jobs" provided a step-by-step action program to guide organizations signed up to participate in EOF programs: obtain information about the women searching for work from state employment offices; then, contact chambers of commerce, boards of trade, and other employer groups to determine shortage occupations; locate vocational training programs that train workers for those shortage occupations; and, finally, identify adult education programs to set up additional classes for mature women.[101]

The "community-action" rhetoric notwithstanding, the Women's Bureau not only established the EOF program but also coordinated the activities of private organizations behind the scenes in several ways: it designed and mailed registration cards, arranged for panel speakers and participating organizations, provided press kits to the local news media, and supplied all information distributed at the meeting. Staff members often organized inaugural community meetings for a planned EOF event and remained in the community to make suggestions and provide information. For example, Marguerite Zapoleon, involved in the early planning meetings for a Miami, Florida, EOF, prompted organizers to offer a sponsorship role to a variety of organizations, including labor, religious, and black women's organizations.[102] It was not unusual for the Women's Bureau to require final approval of every aspect of EOF planning from the location to program content.[103] In addition, Washington coordinated EOF publicity—a publicity campaign accompanied each event. To spark interest in the event beforehand, the Program, Planning, and Analysis Division sent out a press kit that included a feature story by Alice Leopold to every designated newspaper, radio, and television person, as well as to the publicity chairmen of local women's and civic organizations. The Department of Labor bolstered this effort by sending out a national press release, which it followed up with a local press conference the day of the forum.[104]

Public information and publicity became even more important to the Women's Bureau's program after departmental restructuring diminished the research mission, and Leopold took advantage of television to reach as many people as possible. Not only did she promote the EOFs by frequent appearances on talk shows, but also advertised them by purchasing one-minute television spots. Female media professionals—including Edythe Fern Melrose of WXYZ-TV in Detroit, president of the American Women in Radio and Television; Doris Corwith, public service director for the National Broadcasting Service; and Esther Von Wagoner, a Washington correspondent for NBC—helped write the commercial scripts. The typical script began with an opening by Alice Leopold, followed by an introduction from a woman who had taken part in organizing an EOF explaining what her community had done for the older woman worker "with the cooperation of the BPW, Altrusa, Pilot, and other women's service clubs," and ended with an appearance by an older woman entrant to the labor market "to tell her story."[105] The idea to relate a success story of an older woman returning to work came from Washington, D.C., organizers of one of the first Earning Opportunities Forums. The District of Columbia group working with the bureau's staff on the television spots rejected a proposal to include a famous person in favor of highlighting the employment needs of "average Mrs. America."[106] A spot popular with the staff featured a Chinese woman typist who turns from her typewriter to show a picture of the son she is putting through college.[107] The television spots definitely struck a chord with the average mature woman; each forum attracted approximately four hundred job seekers and generated a flood of letters from women seeking advice.[108]

Constrained by a limited budget, the Women's Bureau obtained funding for these commercials from shared advertising arrangements with women's and civic organizations, and especially businesses. Staffers actively sought support from the Chambers of Commerce and the National Association of Manufacturers, a practice that probably irked traditional allies. Careful not to suggest that the Department of Labor endorsed products, commercials ended with a subtle promotion of the cosponsor. A typical example included an ending such as, "This spot has been brought to you as a public service by the Women's Bureau of the United States Department of Labor in cooperation with the John Jones National Bank."[109] Publicity staffer Alice Anderson also tried to get free production services from the networks as part of public service duties.[110] The publicity project yielded several television commercials sent to stations throughout the country.

An equally significant partnership between the Women's Bureau and the National Manpower Council of Columbia University's Graduate School of Business publicized womanpower policies. As president of Columbia University, Dwight D. Eisenhower had created the Manpower Council to make an ongoing study of the manpower problem. One two-year study focused on female workers. The published results, *Womanpower*, had the Women's Bureau's fingerprints all over it. Even though the research function had been severely circumscribed, the federal agency remained the national clearinghouse for information on women's status. A cadre of experts still collected data in the interest of policymaking, and *Womanpower* would not have been possible without their assistance. As a consequence, policy recommendations generated from the study and a subsequent Manpower Council conference on married working women—equity in training, hiring, and promotion; equal pay for equal work; attention to part-time employees; child care services; and an increase in funding for vocational training—mirrored the Women's Bureau's program and policy partnership with women's organizations.[111]

Presentation of *Womanpower* to President Eisenhower by Secretary of Labor James Mitchell placed a federal imperative on the recommendations, which generated extensive media coverage. Five hundred and fifty-two newspapers in forty-seven states ran at least one article on *Womanpower,* and 250 editorials analyzing the policy recommendations appeared throughout the country. Newspapers and magazines covered the lack of representation of women in professional fields especially, such as this comment from the Anniston, *Alabama Star:* "The Council has posed a great challenge in its finding that of all young women capable of absorbing a college education, only one-fourth were graduated from college, and only one out of every 300 capable of earning a degree of Doctor of Philosophy did so."[112] The report's finding that most women would work outside of their homes for twenty-five years also received attention. The Jamaica, New York, *Long Island Press* mused that the two women on the Manpower Council did not attend the White House ceremony because they were probably working.[113]

The Women's Bureau's fortieth anniversary conference in 1960 emphasized women's achievements and essential contributions to the economy. Even so, long-standing ally Olya Margolin, Washington representative for the National Council of Jewish Women, found the event depressing because the anniversary festivities ignored women in industry. Program panelists from personnel, business, and academia annoyed Margolin. To her, the entire program represented nothing more than a publicity event: "It is perfectly possible that this conference was as disappointing to Mrs. Leopold as it was to me. I think her primary purpose was for a great deal of newspaper publicity for herself, but the couple of stories I saw in the Washington Post hardly mentioned her."[114] The Eisenhower administration's public relations emphasis that so frustrated Margolin contributed to women's organizations' inability to improve women's civic and economic status through federal legislation.

Despite failed attempts to pass the Equal Rights Amendment and equal pay legislation, the public service activities of women's organizations prepared women for assertion of political authority by the 1960s. Susan Ware argues that "groups such as the LWV and the PTA created public roles for women denied access to the usual sources of power."[115] Susan Lynn and Susan Levine make similar arguments about the function of the AAUW and YWCA respectively. These organizations provided locations where women with leisure time could study the issues and assume leadership positions denied them in mainstream institutions. Professional activists employed by these organizations remained active, too. The Women's Bureau's placement program offered additional public service activities that maintained organizational commitments to working women. Thus, womanpower initiatives represented continuity between the women's economic agenda advocated by Frieda Miller and renewed legislative activism initiated by President John F. Kennedy's appointee to head the Women's Bureau, Esther Peterson. Civil service employees in the Women's Bureau, like the stalwart Alice Morrison, remained to reintroduce commitments to active policy formation in the 1960s. The next chapter explains why women's organizations joined the Women's Bureau in avowed feminist activism not possible in the 1950s.

CHAPTER 3

Bureaucratic Activism in the New Frontier

Esther Peterson's
Public Policy Goals, 1961–1964

LOOKING BACK on her tenure as Women's Bureau director from 1961 to 1964 in the mid-1980s, Esther Peterson justified her efforts to revive fellow social-safety-netter Frieda Miller's legislative program, including opposition to the Equal Rights Amendment, in the language of partisan politics: "The fact that the predominately Republican women who supported an Equal Rights Amendment in 1960 were not willing to work with us on bread and butter issues like equal pay and minimum wages did not encourage our support for a Constitutional amendment that could well do away with the basic protections we had already won on the state level."[1] Peterson considered the privileged women in the pro-ERA National Woman's Party the "Old Frontier," and her version of the New Frontier meant adjusting the Women's Bureau's public policy goals toward improving the wages of low-income women, especially black women.[2] Still, she did not abandon Alice Leopold's employment placement initiatives because working women remained vital to economic growth. In John F. Kennedy's administration, however, the bureau's womanpower initiatives reflected the resurgence of political liberalism endorsing collective action and government intervention to solve social problems as an alternative to the personal solutions of the 1950s social ethic. Regional employment conferences and the President's Commission on the Status of Women provided institutional frameworks for deliberation of economic policies promoted by the Kennedy administration that defined women as an economically disadvantaged group. The resulting cooperative arrangements among professional activists in labor unions, state labor bureaus, and women's organizations led to a return to a gendered ideology that demanded a government response to women's issues.

New organizational mandates empowered the Women's Bureau to lay claim as a public advocate for women's interests within and outside of the federal government, yet Peterson did not foresee a role for the agency in antidiscrimination enforcement. The Women's Bureau did not administer the 1963 Equal Pay Act because Peterson did not fight to get additional bureaucratic territory for an agency she considered to be an anachronism too vulnerable to budget cuts to be a capable administrator of a federal law. On the other hand, the agency's pivotal role in organizing employment conferences, the PCSW, and the institutions created by the PCSW (the Citizens' Advisory Council on the Status of Women, the Interdepartmental Committee on the Status of Women, and state commissions on the status of women) made it part of the "bureaucratic strand" of the modern women's movement.[3] National forums and permanent advisory bodies brought various organizations and activists together, revealed and publicized discrimination, and created policies that raised expectations for social change. Nevertheless, the bureau's activities remained advisory and bolstering, not administrative. Paradoxically, Peterson, one of Mary Anderson's and Frieda Miller's staunchest allies, did not help the bureau abandon a history of moral persuasion for enforcement, and, as a result, left it vulnerable to the vagaries of party politics and public attitudes about the status of women.

As a lobbyist for the AFL-affiliated Amalgamated Clothing Workers of America after World War II, Peterson joined a network of New Deal Democrats in Washington, including Frieda Miller and John F. Kennedy. The Amalgamated's all-male lobbying staff, uncomfortable with a woman in their midst, asked CIO president Phil Murray, "What are we going to do with Esther?" One staffer said, "Give her to Kennedy; he won't amount to anything."[4] Representative John F. Kennedy, who, as Alonzo Hamby writes, "adopted the urban 'bread and butter liberalism' of the New Deal coalition," impressed Peterson with his sympathies toward working people.[5] She found another policy alliance and a refuge from male-dominated union politics in the bureau's Trade Union Advisory Committee, which brought together a small network of professional activists concerned with women's issues.

In order to wield more influence in Congress with the Republican Dwight D. Eisenhower in the White House, liberal Democrats collaborated with interest groups, especially organized labor and civil rights organizations, to establish the Democratic Advisory Council. Kennedy, then a senator and a member of the Senate Labor Committee, renewed his ties to Peterson, a lobbyist with the Industrial Union Department of the AFL-CIO.[6] Progressive policy alliances during the Democrats' wilderness years formed the core of Kennedy's presidential campaign in 1960, which promoted federal activism in civil rights, education, health care, worker retraining, and economic planning. Proponents of the "New Economics"—a theory that championed consistent government intervention in the economy to maintain full employment—found a place in the Kennedy camp. These policy recommendations, in contrast to Eisenhower's ideology of limited government, helped put over Kennedy's election strategy to capture the "urban-industrial political coalition" of African Americans, Catholics, and organized labor.[7]

As president, Kennedy provided access to members of the urban-industrial coalition by writing executive orders creating commissions and committees to study social problems. Kennedy's close margin of victory over Richard M. Nixon precluded the election mandate necessary to rally Congress, still dominated by a coalition of southern Democrats and Republicans that had stymied Harry S. Truman, around the Democratic Advisory Council's legislative program.[8] Therefore, executive government formulated policy in other ways. Representatives from interest groups, who came in through the back door of the White House in advisory capacities, expanded the staff of the chief executive. Newly appointed secretary of labor, Arthur J. Goldberg, a former labor lawyer with the United Steelworkers Union, also brought in a staff representing diverse ethnic, religious, geographic, and economic backgrounds.[9] Even before the inauguration, seven task forces prepared an administrative response to social problems, and these committees served as sources for staff.[10] Well-prepared to begin presidential leadership, Kennedy exerted more control over appointments to federal bureaucracies than his predecessors Truman and Eisenhower.[11] Commission and committee deliberations brought auxiliary dividends in allowing the president to manipulate public opinion. As Otis Graham points out, both Kennedy and Johnson sought to invigorate the presidency "by expanding staff, manipulating public opinion to bring pressure constantly to bear on congressmen and bureaucrats."[12] This strategy led to the passage of legislation aimed at ensuring full employment: the Area Redevelopment Act, the Manpower Training and Redevelopment Act, and a higher minimum wage with expanded coverage.

The ascendancy of political liberalism within the Kennedy administration and changes in the status of women challenged the suburban social ethic that dictated the programmatic goals of several women's organizations. According to Alice Kessler-Harris, "wage earning became the life style of all kinds of women—the educated, the married, the affluent as well as the needy."[13] Declining birth rates before the discovery of the birth control pill in 1960 and an increase in the number of bachelor's degrees awarded to women between 1960 and 1965 signaled women's shifting allegiance from home to work.[14] The AAUW eased membership restrictions to lure increasing numbers of college graduates, including black women, into the organization. While the AAUW remained an emblem of middle-class comfort during the 1960s, the membership did become more heterogeneous compared to previous years. Marguerite Rawalt, active in the Business and Professional Women's Clubs and a PCSW member, experienced a similar political awakening. As her biographer, Judith Peterson, explains, "her understanding of 'women's issues' was expanding beyond the narrow concerns of professional women. Now her speeches argued for public child care, equal pay for working women, and job training for women."[15] The AAUW representative to the PCSW, Pauline Tompkins, brought to bear a sympathy toward working women's issues that the BPW and LWV shared, pressing for equal pay, federally subsidized child care, and reform of state laws denying married women economic autonomy. Tompkins and her successor, Blanche Hinman Dow, AAUW president from 1963 to 1967, presided over structural reforms designed to overcome "branch passivity."[16]

Women's groups from the urban-industrial coalition, shut out of policy formation during the Eisenhower administration because of their unwavering liberalism, also embraced political action. Reflecting organized labor's interest in the political participation of the rank and file after devastating legislative defeats in the late 1940s and 1950s, the United Automobile Workers' Women's Department encouraged its members during the 1960s to get politically in-volved.[17] Historian of the National Council of Jewish Women, Faith Rogow, suggests that the legacy of the Holocaust inspired members to protect civil rights and civil liberties even in an era of conservatism. The NCJW's alliance with the burgeoning civil rights movement led to an FBI investigation of its activities during the Red Scare.[18] The civil rights movement rekindled progressive alli-ances even before Kennedy's election. The national board of the NCJW, undeterred by McCarthyism, passed a resolution support-ing integration in 1955, the same year as the Montgomery bus boy-cott. Ironically, the death of prominent leader Mary McLeod Bethune that year left the National Council of Negro Women in limbo. Paula Giddings argues that newly installed NCNW presi-dent and YWCA employee Dorothy Height, aware of the clubby orientation of the NCNW in the 1950s as black professional wom-en eschewed political action, set out in 1958 to build coalitions with organizations she admired as committed to social justice: the National Council of Jewish Women, Church Women United, the National Council of Catholic Women, and the YWCA.[19] The YWCA retreated from gender-identified politics during the 1950s, yet it pursued civil rights activism consistent with charters support-ing integration passed by national conventions during the 1940s.[20] Student YWCA members, involved in direct action campaigns in the South, received legal and financial support from the National YWCA.[21]

Women's organizations' keen interest in the direction of poli-cymaking within the Women's Bureau is evident in the support and opposition to Esther Peterson's appointment as director. Liberal-leaning organizations endorsed Kennedy's choice to succeed Repub-lican Alice Leopold. Actually, according to Peterson, labor union women organized a campaign to place her in the Women's Bureau: "Some of the union girls began talking about getting me appointed. Then a lot of the women began organizing (Clara Beyers, Louise Stilt, Ann Draker and others). They had a luncheon and wanted to know if I wouldn't let them propose me for the Women's Bureau."[22] Offered a choice of positions in the Kennedy administration, including a job with the United Nations, Peterson chose the bureau instead because she had a "labor union base."[23] Conversely, groups encouraged by Alice Leopold's womanpower policies and abandonment of active promotion of protective labor legislation opposed the nomination of a director with such close ties to organized labor. The Business and Professional Women's Clubs, an important ally on the career placement front, designated another candidate for the job, Catherine Fitzgerald. Fitzgerald, a former deputy commissioner of the New York State Commerce Department, chaired the BPW's national career advancement committee.[24] Clearly, the BPW sought a seamless transition from a Republican to a Democratic administration in the area of national career-planning initiatives for professional women. Helen H. Kokes, president of the Nebraska Business and Professional Women's Clubs, wrote to Lawrence F. O'Brien, special assistant to the president, that "appointing Esther Peterson to the Women's Bureau did not specially impress us as a gesture of recognition."[25]

The National Woman's Party, a vociferous opponent to the appointment of the former labor lobbyist, argued that Peterson, who had testified against the ERA on behalf of the AFL-CIO at the Democratic platform hearings in 1960, "followed the footsteps of Walter Reuther."[26] NWP national chairman Emma Guffy Miller, herself a Democrat, nevertheless bemoaned the resurgence of interest group politics within the Labor Department: "It seems very unfortunate that the administration appoints a woman to head the Women's Division of the Labor Department who is antagonistic to the movement of the freedom of women. They all seem to be controlled by labor who is fearful that if women gain equality under the law they will take the jobs men seem to think they only are entitled to."[27]

Guffy Miller failed to see that the White House's reliance on outside groups for policy formation offered one site where women's organizations could focus attention on employment rights. Susan Levine describes the ascendancy of the liberal agenda as a positive change that enabled women's organizations, on the defensive during the 1950s, to begin to build political coalitions again: "Long isolated by cold-war caution and historically divided over ERA, women's groups began to reunite for a common cause. The 1960s, then, witnessed not so much a 'rebirth' of feminism as its legitimization as part of the 'mainstream liberal' agenda."[28] Within months of Kennedy's inauguration, Goldberg and Peterson organized a one-day conference for women's organizations to unveil action plans in the following areas: collection of evidence of unequal pay to support the administration's pending equal pay bill; studies on part-time employment and displacement due to automation; support of community-based training programs provided by the recently passed Area Redevelopment Act, which Kennedy's economic planners hoped would be a permanent remedy for rampant unemployment in areas losing industrial jobs; and participation in upcoming bureau-sponsored regional employment conferences. Goldberg made a personal plea to women's organizations for educational campaigns to convince the public that women needed to work, because some members of Congress questioned the accuracy of employment figures including women. The conferees countered with requests for a comprehensive study of discrimination against women and a centralized publication reporting the bureau's activities—an indication that women's organizations had begun to disavow personal solutions to social problems.[29]

For Peterson and Goldberg, following the tenets of the New Economics, discrimination would disappear in a robust economy that put everyone to work. A stagnant economy victimized all workers. Alice Kessler-Harris suggests that Kennedy linked employment rights to an expanded economy, and that Secretary Goldberg, who shared this view, "tied opportunities for women directly to a healthy economy rather than to human rights."[30] In numerous speeches to women's and union groups, Peterson presented the administration's position, as she did in a speech to a conference on working women at Iowa State University in 1963: "Unless the economy expands and we are able to provide the jobs for all who need or want to work, women will continue to be considered marginal workers, expected to work at substandard wages and to give up their jobs at cut-back time."[31]

A focus on full employment provided a different and compelling rationale for reviving state and federal labor legislation—maximum hours for overtime and higher minimum wages for both men and women stimulated the economy by increasing purchasing power. Thus, Peterson promoted labor legislation as part of a national economic policy: "In successfully pushing an increased and extended minimum wage bill through Congress, the Administration is raising the level of pay of some of our lowest salaried workers in order that they may achieve a more nearly adequate standard of living, participate more fully in our economy and thereby help stimulate our national growth."[32] Similarly, she supported the extension of unemployment compensation insurance as a key to economic growth because it would generate "$1 billion in purchasing power."[33]

Peterson's elevation to assistant secretary of labor for Labor Standards in 1961 allowed her to direct legislative efforts in the labor standards area. Public pressure to appoint more women to higher-level government positions no doubt influenced Secretary Goldberg's decision to create another assistant secretary post.[34] Whatever the reason, the position gave Peterson the authority she needed to restore functions suspended by the Eisenhower administration, such as conferences for state minimum wage administrators and women's organizations designed to stimulate grassroots movements for state minimum wage laws and active policy formation.[35] In its annual report for fiscal year 1961 the Labor Department made a distinction between the federalism of the New Frontier and the states' rights orientation of the previous administration: "This year, the President's proposals asked for an acknowledgment of the national character and national responsibility of the problems of unemployment and recession."[36] Successful commitments to national responsibility included amendments to the Fair Labor Standards Act (FLSA) raising the minimum wage and extending coverage to previously unregulated occupations, including the several female-dominated service and retail jobs exempted since 1938, and passage of state minimum wage laws with amendments providing overtime pay.[37]

The demands of the civil rights movement furnished additional reasons for state maximum hours and minimum wage legislation, as African American women remained in the lowest-paid occupations still exempted from federal laws. The 1961 FLSA amendments, in a compromise with congressional Republicans, failed to include the hotel, laundry, and agricultural jobs black women dominated. The persistence of loopholes in the FLSA explains why the Women's Bureau returned to active promotion of state minimum wage and maximum hours legislation. Until additional amendments to the FLSA could be added by congressional action, state labor laws promised to improve the wages of black women. Peterson established a Special Projects Branch to effect the inclusion of African American women in wage legislation.[38]

Regional employment conferences in Michigan, California, Massachusetts, and Tennessee revivified "Reconversion Blueprint" coalitions for state minimum wage and equal pay legislation. For example, the planning committee for the first regional conference at Michigan State University included representatives from the American Association of University Women, the National Council of Jewish Women, the YWCA, the UAW's Women's Department, and the Michigan State Department of Labor. The economist Dan Kruger from Michigan State University came to Washington to finalize an agenda focusing on legislation, education and training, child care, and migratory workers with the Women's Bureau's staff. Information kits for conferees included government publications on state minimum wage laws.[39] Some participants in the Michigan conference criticized labor union domination, though. One respondent objected to the attention paid to interest groups: "This is too partisan—after all the USA is made up of many varieties of people and tolerance should be extended to others than Catholics, Jews, labor leaders, and Negroes."[40]

Despite criticisms charging interest group domination, field representatives continued to direct conference planners to focus on topics related to labor legislation whenever possible. A committee for a working women's conference sponsored by Mount Holyoke College narrowed down a list of five topics to two—equal pay legislation and training—during a meeting on December 6, 1961, much to the delight of staffer Mildred Barber, who supported choices paralleling the Labor Department's legislative goals and manpower programs.[41] Meanwhile, from Washington, Peterson tried to downplay federal involvement by echoing Alice Leopold's community voluntarism rhetoric: "Each conference, although sponsored by the Women's Bureau, State and Educational Agencies, is primarily a community project. A steering committee, composed of representatives of groups concerned with the welfare of working women, organizes and directs the conference."[42]

Professional bureaucrats did not always defer to the grassroots, however. Aware of the regional conferences' reputation for advocating minimum wage and equal pay legislation, the Nashville, Tennessee, Chamber of Commerce refused to sanction any meeting considering labor legislation. At the same time, state labor officials cautioned field representative Augusta Clawson that women's organizations in Nashville would not participate in a conference involving labor unions. Indeed, Clawson, on the scene in October 1961 to organize a regional employment conference, discovered a "conservative element which would like the conference, but has some apprehension—in some cases real concern—that too much emphasis on minimum wage or equal pay legislation or even on union participation might repeal [*sic*] a considerable portion of the community."[43] Leaders of women's groups meeting with Clawson preferred programs on worker retraining, youth guidance, and child care. The local Business and Professional Women's Club alone sought a legislative program. Although the state labor commissioner, William H. Parham, urged "finesse when presenting the labor point of view," he did not suggest abandoning the legislative agenda entirely.[44] Clawson agreed, writing to Peterson: "It would be my considered judgment that Nashville would be an appropriate place for such a conference and that the program be planned with certain sensitivity, realizing this element, yet facing the fact that there are problems and conditions which need changing."[45]

Regional conferences sometimes became places for groups with opposing positions on labor legislation to share ideas and to work out compromises. Although conference planners in Los Angeles favored a network of unions and state labor departments, field representative Phillis Basile recruited commentators with a "neutral background" to moderate a discussion on homemakers and workers.[46] Panelists included people involved in youth guidance, home management, child care, and workforce reentry for mature women. A session called "Opportunities and Protection" included participants from low-skilled and low-paying jobs, management, and the professions. Arizona and California representatives came to the Los Angeles conference prepared to discuss controversial state maximum hours laws. Corporations with defense contracts in Arizona argued that performance requirements on bids required women in skilled occupations to work overtime. As a result, some women's organizations aligned with employers to challenge maximum hours restrictions in the state.[47] A member of the Arizona Industrial Commission hoped to meet with opponents of maximum hours laws to work out a compromise. Representatives from the California branch of the Business and Professional Women's Clubs, also concerned that restrictive hours laws affected the advancement of women in supervisory positions, attended to plead their case to labor groups. All the while, Phillis Basile hoped that the California women would accept a compromise amending the California Fair Labor Standards Act to cover both men and women in maximum hours provisions providing for time-and-a-half for overtime.[48]

Regional employment conferences functioned as just one of several means of collaboration between the federal government and labor unions, state labor departments, and women's organizations. Prohibited from engaging in practical politics, the Women's Bureau relied on confederates to lobby for its legislative program. Toward that end, Peterson restored an alliance with the National Committee for Equal Pay, which had been alienated by the Labor Department's refusal to endorse Representative Edith Green's equal pay bills in the mid-1950s. The NCEP then provided witnesses for congressional hearings on the administration's equal pay bill.[49] Renewed commitments to federal legislation put the Trade Union Advisory Committee disbanded by Leopold back in business; this network supplied research and professional lobbying resources from trade unions. In addition, Mildred Barber suggested reconvening a women's advisory committee "to advise and assist our program."[50]

At Peterson's behest, a small committee composed of women with sympathies to organized labor drafted a proposal for a commission on the status of women. Helen Betholt of the Communication Workers of America; Bureau staffer and black trade unionist Dollie Lowther Robinson; and Katherine Ellickson, assistant director of the Department of Social Security, who met Peterson when they both worked for the AFL, worked on the draft proposal. NCJW lobbyist Olya Margolin, no longer on the margins in federal policymaking, also participated in the deliberations. The original plan, written by Ellickson, put the commission in the Women's Bureau as authorized by the secretary of labor, not the president. However, Margolin did not believe that pro-ERA groups would accept any subsequent recommendations from an assemblage functioning under the auspices of the Labor Department.[51] Peterson did not want a Labor Department–authorized commission either, and she and Goldberg decided to draft an executive order for a presidential commission modeled on Executive Order 10925, which had formed the President's Committee on Equal Employment Opportunity. On December 14, 1961,

Kennedy signed Executive Order 10980, creating the President's Commission on the Status of Women to be administered by the Labor Department.

Perhaps the decision to use the civil rights order format indicates that the civil rights movement's success in getting a federal response to racial discrimination in employment heightened expectations among female activists for a similar response with regard to women. While Peterson's subcommittee drafted a commission proposal, Muriel Ferris, legislative assistant to Senator Philip A. Hart, Democrat from Michigan, urged the White House staff to address the politically embarrassing fact that women were underemployed in the federal government by issuing an executive order on women similar to Executive Order 10925.[52] Ellickson, in a memo stating the purpose of a commission, expressed a similar sentiment: "Just as the President has done in the field of race discrimination, so he must carry over into the field of women."[53] Dollie Robinson took the race analogy a step further, suggesting to UAW women prior to the formation of the National Organization for Women that feminists needed an "NAACP for women."[54]

Further deliberations on the commission's membership and mission within the Labor Department considered interest group politics. To make sure that the commission functioned as part of the executive government, not just the Labor Department, Peterson insisted on cabinet-level representation, including John Macy, chairman of the Civil Service Commission, Robert F. Kennedy, the attorney general of the United States, and the secretaries of Commerce, Labor, Agriculture, and Health, Education, and Welfare. Moreover, she assiduously recruited individuals representing interest groups already involved in policy formation within the Kennedy administration: "And I very definitely wanted industry, labor, women, all people who were concerned, and I did not want a women's commission. I wanted people who were in a position to act."[55] But more important, she sought to control the PCSW's membership for political reasons: "I wanted to have the votes. I thought it was very necessary to be sure we had enough people there who would vote along the lines that I thought the Commission should go."[56] Consequently, Pennsylvania governor David L. Lawrence failed to persuade Kennedy to appoint National Woman's Party chairman Emma Guffy Miller.[57] Instead, Peterson relied on long-standing policy partners: Viola Hymes, president of the National Council of Jewish Women; Marguerite Rawalt, past president of the National Federation of Business and Professional Women's Clubs and the token pro-ERA member; Margaret J. Mealy, executive director of the National Council of Catholic Women; Dorothy Height, president of the National Council of Negro Women; and Mary Callahan, a member of the executive board of the International Union of Electrical, Radio, and Machine Workers. Despite this interest group–focused representation, Assistant Secretary of Labor Daniel Patrick Moynihan, a member of an informal Labor Department subcommittee reviewing PCSW plans, thought that the commission list failed to guarantee diversity because it lacked wide geographical distribution and representation from Spanish-speaking groups.[58]

Seven PCSW committees drafting policies to achieve equity in education, employment, social insurance and taxes, and civil and political status, each chaired by a commission member, involved additional representatives from interest groups and think tanks largely, but not exclusively, representing the urban-industrial coalition; more than one hundred people contributed to the PCSW's recommendations through this committee structure. The collection of individuals from disparate economic and educational backgrounds on the Protective Labor Legislation Committee greatly impressed trade unionist Mary Callahan: "There were people with whom I had never expected to sit down at a roundtable. . . . Then, to sit with an editor from the *Ladies' Home Journal* and somebody from Radcliffe College and other people who had their Ph.D.'s in all kinds of things. Even some merchants and people from great big department stores."[59] Convened to consider bias in state laws, particularly in the areas of jury service and property rights, the Committee on Civil and Political Rights included Yale law professor Pauli Murray, appointed on the recommendation of her friend Dollie Robinson. Murray, who had been interested in women's rights since the 1940s but had never worked on these issues until her appointment to the PCSW subcommittee, met with and got to know representatives from the Business and Professional Women's Clubs, the League of Women Voters, and the General Federation of Women's Clubs.[60] Policy partners from the American Association of University Women and the AFL-CIO served on the Education Committee along with experts from academia and federal and state governments.[61]

The proliferation of study groups in order to involve larger numbers of political allies had the unintended consequence of coopting some of the Labor Department's goals. Just as in the case of the regional employment conferences, intense scrutiny of women's legal and economic status provided a communication network that allowed participants to explore various prescriptions for social change. For instance, the inevitable negotiations within the Civil and Political Rights Committee on the Equal Rights Amendment allowed for independent actions that brought equal rights feminism into consideration. To ensure unanimous support for final recommendations, members of the committee worked hard to accommodate Marguerite Rawalt's pro-ERA views. Pauli Murray described the deliberative process that succeeded in building a consensus: "We spent hours with her [Rawalt], struggling over phraseology, and finally settled on a sentence that read: 'In view of this constitutional approach, the Committee does not take a position in favor of the proposed equal rights amendment at this time.'"[62] Rawalt succeeded in adding more temperate language opposing the ERA with the help of an unlikely ally, Margaret Mealy, executive director of the National Council of Catholic Women. Mealy opposed the ERA but respected Rawalt, whom she got to know during the deliberations. When Rawalt proposed the following additional language in the recommendation, that "the Commission believes that constitutional changes need not *now* be sought," Mealy supported it.[63]

At other times, rising expectations about a government response to sex discrimination led to the creation of feminist manifestos in minority reports dissenting from the moderate PCSW report *American Women*. Caroline Davis, director of the UAW Women's Department and a member of the Committee on Private Employment, condemned the committee's unwillingness to push for a strongly worded executive order prohibiting sex discrimination by employers with federal contracts. Muriel Ferris, another committee member, shared Davis's outrage. Davis's colleague in the UAW Women's Department, Dorothy Haener, who believed that the PCSW was the "forerunner" of the women's movement because "it gave us a chance to know each other," nevertheless found the moderate tone of the final policy recommendations disappointing.[64] A minority view also surfaced on the Protective Labor Legislation Committee, where some members objected to restrictive maximum hours laws and sought compromise language. The subsequent endorsement of state maximum hours laws in the absence of overtime provisions exempted professional and executive women. Even with this concession to the equal rights perspective, commissioner Margaret Hickey expressed frustration at the committee's retention of language supporting separate labor legislation for women.[65] Another minority report even considered abortion.

At the same time, the Kennedy administration's concern with the economic ramifications of women remaining an underutilized resource mitigated against upholding traditionalist views. The idea that the country could ill-afford another generation of women condemned to meaningless lives at middle age won out over Moynihan's suggestion that the PCSW should instead push for a stronger economy "in which men made enough money that their women can stay home and raise their family."[66] Kennedy's announcement of Executive Order 10980 focused on women as workers: "Women should not be a marginal group to be employed periodically, only to be denied opportunity to satisfy their needs and aspirations when unemployment rises or a war ends."[67] Indeed, the final re-port's "invitation to action"—bolstered by facts, figures, and conclu-sions from the Council of Economic Advisors indicating that "the country's productive capacity exceeded its actual output by $170 billion, or almost $1,000 per person in the United States"— defined women as important economic contributors.[68]

In the New Frontier, government bore the responsibility for creating opportunities for productive lives through instituting sound economic planning and progressive public policies. Therefore, PCSW recommendations placed the burden on local, state, and federal governments to improve the status of women. Legislative recommendations focused on expansion of governmental enforcement authority in the workplace primarily through federal and state labor laws providing for overtime, extension of unemployment compensation coverage, maternity leave benefits, and equal pay for comparable work. Exhortations for presidential executive orders and directives in particular followed a pattern of social change already practiced by the White House. One ensuing order created a cabinet-level officer to execute the recommendations within the federal government. Kennedy also directed cabinet heads to consider women for high-level federal appointments. Another recommendation sought an executive order to ensure standards of equal employment opportunity by contractors doing business with the federal government.[69]

The commission's balancing act between liberalism's interest in expanding state authority and the equal rights perspective of prominent policy partners is most clearly manifested in the summary report of the Protective Labor Legislation Committee. Nearly all members of this committee, according to member Mary Callahan, came prepared to critically review discriminatory aspects of extant protective labor laws.[70] Subsequent deliberations indicated ways to amend laws restricting women's employment opportunities without taking the state out of the workplace through outright repeal. Instead, policy formation should be flexible enough to distinguish between types of workers, occupations, and shifts. One such proposal advocated additional state laws to protect both men and women from employer abuse and to create services for all employees working the third shift. Another curative for discriminatory state labor legislation would be the establishment of regulatory commissions within the federal Labor Department and state labor bureaus to examine job-related qualifications on a case-by-case basis.[71] Similarly, rather than retreat from maximum hours and minimum wage legislation, state legislatures should amend existing laws or introduce new legislation protecting both men and women.

Seeking to avoid criticism from "equal righters," Peterson used the PCSW's recommendations to get policies on women's issues integrated throughout the federal government "so I could go to the various agencies and say, 'This idea is the result of a recommendation, the Commission's. This isn't just Esther Peterson talking.' We needed so badly to change the bureaucratic approach to things, to have a basis for the changes."[72] Using his position as attorney general, Robert F. Kennedy removed a legal barrier to equal opportunity by prohibiting federal offices from requesting men or women only. The Pentagon eliminated the quota system for female officers. Improvements in tax laws allowing for deductions for child care appeared in the administration's tax legislation. The Department of Health, Education, and Welfare agreed to establish child care facilities in federally subsidized housing and promised to convene conferences for groups engaged in organizing child care centers. Research projects advocated by PCSW committees often appeared on the agendas of cabinet-level departments, and departments paid to publish research reports.[73]

Neither cabinet-level involvement in implementing PCSW recommendations nor the emergence of grassroots movements for state commissions on the status of women changed Peterson's mind about the Women's Bureau's limited effectiveness in policy formation. BPW vice president Virginia Allen suggested state commissions on the federal model during a meeting with Peterson and special assistant to the PCSW Mary Hilton.[74] With Kennedy's blessing, the BPW began state organizing campaigns with the help of the Women's Bureau in 1963. Ever sensitive to states' rights issues, Peterson, in her letters to individuals interested in state commissions, emphasized that the BPW led the burgeoning state commission movement. In fact, Peterson envisioned the bureau as functioning solely as the staff arm, not the leader, of new women's rights institutions. Her plan to deprive the Women's Bureau of independent action included transferring extant research, publicity, and legislative functions to other Labor Department bureaus and divisions with expertise and resources and making the director a civil-service functionary rather than a political appointee. These proposed organizational adjustments would certainly mollify members of Congress, who year after year complained that the Women's Bureau duplicated the functions of the Bureaus of Labor Standards, Labor Statistics, and the Office of the Solicitor.

Peterson's unwillingness to give the Women's Bureau enforcement authority is evident in her support for compromise equal pay legislation similar to the alternatives to Edith Green's bills promoted by the Eisenhower administration. The Kennedy administration's support for Republican Frances Bolton's original compromise to appease business interests, an equal pay amendment to the Fair Labor Standards Act, which would utilize existing, less punitive, enforcement mechanisms in the Labor Department and exempt several job categories, did not please members of the National Committee for Equal Pay. In 1956 NCEP affiliates rejected Bolton's compromise in dramatic fashion by calling a press conference to publicly support Congresswoman Green's commitment to expanded enforcement, including a role for the Women's Bureau, and broader categories of coverage possible by amending the National Labor Relations Act. No doubt stunned that Democrats would support such a compromise in 1962, Olya Margolin expressed her frustration with the Labor Department's turnaround in a letter to her colleague Helen Raebeck: "They [the U.S. Chamber of Commerce] also will propose a series of amendments, but the bill is so weak that no amendments can really hurt it very much, except a substitute of identical for comparable. I understand that the Department of Labor will not accept this amendment, but then who knows, they might negotiate a surrender as they did on some other proposals."[75]

To get the bill out of the House Committee on Education and Labor with a unanimous report, the Kennedy administration acted just as Margolin predicted. Committee debates offered additional weakening amendments, including Katharine St. George's amendment changing the bill's language from "equal pay for comparable work" to "equal pay for equal work." Peterson, discussing the compromise language during an interview in 1970, recalled that she was furious with St. George: "If you have work of comparable character—but equal, then you get down to identical, and she really wrecked us. Some of the things that got into the bill have been very difficult. She was really a negative force on the bill. So I had no regard for some of these women. They supported the equal rights amendment but not the equal pay bill."[76] Even so, Peterson, interested in getting a law passed following the momentum created by the PCSW's report, encouraged the Labor Department to accept the compromise language in the end.[77] She reasoned, albeit too optimistically, that even a weak bill had tremendous potential to complement womanpower goals: "By making women's jobs more interchangeable with men's jobs, it tends to increase the job mobility of women, and consequently their value to their employers. It helps remove barriers to women's training and promotion, and serves as an incentive to women to prepare themselves for jobs requiring higher skills, an essential component in our program to meet the manpower needs of a growing U.S. economy."[78]

Early on in the fight for congressional support for equal pay the Women's Bureau staff attempted to parcel out some bureaucratic jurisdiction. Laura Dale drafted a memorandum outlining why the Women's Bureau should administer the law: "Because of

its knowledge of State equal pay law administration and enforcement and its many and varied contacts with voluntary organizations,
the Bureau is the logical agency to promote voluntary compliance
with the equal pay law. Preparation of promotional publications, as
well as regulations and procedures would necessarily require
Women's Bureau technical knowledge."[79] Alice Morrison distributed the memorandum to the staff prior to the November 20, 1961,
meeting to discuss administration of the pending equal pay bill.
Despite Dale's arguments, the staff came to a consensus that the
balance of enforcement authority should reside in the division already overseeing the Fair Labor Standards Act, the Wage, Hour,
and Public Contracts Divisions (WHPC). Alice Morrison and Mary
Robinson suggested that, at the very least, the Women's Bureau
should have a role in convening conciliation hearings and inspec-
tions. Some members of the staff feared that equal pay enforcement, if left to another division, would become a low priority, a
pattern of benign neglect many of them had experienced as the
result of departmental reorganization during the Eisenhower administration.

NCEP activists eventually supported the compromise legislation as well because the Kennedy administration had included them
in policy deliberations. Federal bureaucrats' attention to the goals
of interest groups avoided the divisiveness that resulted from the
Eisenhower administration's acrimonious relationship with the
urban-industrial coalition, a breakdown in women's rights coalition-
building that doomed any positive action on equal pay during the
1950s. Staffers from the WHPC succeeded in convincing Green loy-
alists that a weakened version of the bill established a law that could
be improved upon later. Cynthia Harrison credits the bureau's success in working with interest groups for passage of the Equal Pay
Act of 1963: "The leadership of the Women's Bureau proved cru-
cial. The Bureau forged a compromise by persuading women's
organizations and labor groups to accept a bill lacking features they
had considered vital and by quashing disunity in the administration."[80]

Staffers did not entirely give up on administration of the equal
pay law after Kennedy signed it into law on June 10, 1963, as the
scene shifted to internecine struggles within the Labor Department over dividing jurisdictional plums. Another internal memo on

administrative functions revived Laura Dale's argument that networks with allies in state governments and private organizations furnished mechanisms for education toward voluntary compliance that other bureaus and divisions would have to construct from scratch at a much higher cost. Proposed promotional projects complemented existing womanpower goals. For example, the Women's Bureau wanted the authority to publicize the need for women in the labor force and to initiate studies to evaluate how equal pay affected women's decisions to work or not to work.[81] By proposing several equal pay studies, the Women's Bureau attempted to control the research side of administration as well.[82]

Enforcement compromises left the Women's Bureau in a less than ideal position when pleading for administrative territory, however. Even Peterson, a key player in the politics behind the passage of the Equal Pay Act, had no control over which divisions and bureaus would be awarded research and publicity functions by Secretary of Labor Willard Wirtz. Remarkably, the Women's Bureau had no role in drafting the Labor Department's informational booklet, "Highlights of the Equal Pay Act of 1963," which turned Peterson into a lobbyist for language changes deflecting attention from weaknesses in enforcement to avoid alienating organizations that had worked so long for federal equal pay legislation. As she wrote to Clarence T. Lundquist, administrator of the WHPC, "We shall be grateful for your help in keeping this somewhat 'touchy' situation [compromise on enforcement] in mind, especially during the first year of operation before the law becomes effective and when there will be a good deal of informational material going out."[83]

The battle over administrative territory began in earnest by July when Tom Kouzes, director of the Office of Organization and Management, began circulating equal pay activity analysis reports for comment by heads of divisions and bureaus with a stake in administration. Kouzes's first report denied the Women's Bureau a role in developing administrative procedures and research. Staff member Mary Manning complained: "The presumption that the Women's Bureau will do little basic research or analysis of state experience . . . is inconsistent with its assigned responsibility to afford technical assistance to States, labor unions and women's organizations."[84] In this case, Peterson sided with her staff, offering "amendments" to the draft, not the least of which insisted upon a place in "determining overall general policy" and an expanded research function to analyze the administration of state equal pay laws and to study the implications on hiring and wage differentials with the equal pay law in effect.[85] Additional suggestions more consistent with the Women's Bureau's established mission included public information and education to inform both the public and employers of the law's implications.

The next draft delighted Women's Bureau Deputy Director Beatrice McConnell, who scribbled a message to Alice Morrison: "It seems to me we are 'in' for about everything we requested," but it brought a negative response from the Bureau of Labor Statistics.[86] The equal pay activity analysis circulated to division and bureau heads at the end of July included the Women's Bureau in policy formation, education, and research, although primary responsibilities still related to work with women's organizations. Nevertheless, Philip Arnow, representing the Bureau of Labor Statistics, wrote to Kouzes objecting to a plan that allowed any other bureau or division to conduct studies; other areas did not have the "statistical know-how, trained personnel, or field resources" to carry out actual data collection.[87] Arnow's memo stunned McConnell, who apparently did not receive an invitation to a meeting discussing the BLS's rejection of the new draft.[88]

The subsequent Secretary's Order outlining administrative functions for the four areas affected by the Equal Pay Act—the Women's Bureau, the BLS, the WHPC, and the Solicitor's Office—developed from a slew of activity reports, raised additional concerns about effective administration. Specifically, the order blurred the administrative boundaries between the Women's Bureau and the WHPC. Clarence Lundquist objected to language that placed "functional supervision" of all equal pay activities, including compliance, with the Women's Bureau director.[89] He pleaded with Assistant Secretary for Administration Leo R. Werts in several memos to assign the Women's Bureau to a consultative function only. McConnell fought back. She pressed Werts to go beyond a general statement of functions "giving the Women's Bureau responsibility for 'assisting' or 'participating' in the development of various types of policies and procedures" and issue specific operating guidelines.[90]

In the end, the Women's Bureau did not succeed in getting operating procedures that spelled out new functions justifying significant budget increases. The order retained language that, while acknowledging the Women's Bureau's stake in policy formation, emphasized consultation and review of research programs and policies developed by the WHPC. To make matters worse, Secretary Wirtz assigned research and publicity functions to other bureaus, particularly the Bureau of Labor Statistics. The Solicitor's Office and the WHPC added staff to administer the law. The Equal Pay Act of 1963 did not augment significantly the Women's Bureau's authority or function. Instead, the compromise legislation that tacked equal pay onto existing regulatory mechanisms of the Fair Labor Standards Act put enforcement in the WHPC.

Loopholes in the Equal Pay Act increased the relevance of Representative Howard W. Smith's addition of the word "sex" to the equal employment opportunity section, Title VII, of the Lyndon B. Johnson administration's civil rights bill. Bess Dick, chief of staff of the Judiciary Committee of the House of Representatives, wrote to Peterson seeking the Women's Bureau's position on the Virginia Democrat's amendment. In rejecting the amendment in favor of the administration's original measure, Peterson referred to the PCSW's preference for separate responses to discrimination against women. Moreover, she feared that Smith's tactic would undermine Johnson's civil rights program.[91] Other PCSW activists disagreed with this interpretation. An informal network of former PCSW members kept each other informed about progress on women's rights. When Republican senator Everett Dirksen of Illinois announced his plans to oppose Representative Smith's amendment, Pauli Murray relates that "our little network began to consult frantically by telephone. We hardly knew what strategy to pursue."[92] Marguerite Rawalt, by then active on the Citizens' Advisory Council, suggested that Murray, whom she got to know fairly well through PCSW deliberations, write a memorandum to President Johnson supporting the House's version of the bill. Murray's memo included an argument that civil rights legislation would reinforce the Equal Pay Act of 1963 and a critique of the PCSW's recommendation that separate legislative actions should address sex discrimination.[93] Rawalt sent the memo to Johnson and made copies for senators. Illinois BPW members pressured Dirksen to abandon his objections to the "sex" inclusion. Johnson's eventual support of the House version, to avoid a conference on the bill in the Senate, changed Peterson's mind.[94]

The bureau's investment in Johnson's civil rights policies had its roots in the activities of the National Women's Committee for Civil Rights (NWCCR). President Kennedy made a personal appeal for women's organizations' support for his civil rights program at a national women's conference on that issue put together by the bureau in July 1963. The conference led to the formation of a thirteen-member steering committee to coordinate the civil rights activities of women's organizations committed to following Kennedy's five-point action plan, which included goals to initiate interracial projects on the community level in the South and active support for the administration's civil rights bill. To disguise federal involvement in forming and maintaining the NWCCR, Kennedy staffers made sure that the office would not be housed in any government building. Peterson served as a liaison between the administration and the group, but she pointed out that, although the new committee was created with the blessing of the Women's Bureau, it functioned as a private organization relying on donations and community support to maintain a staff of two.[95]

These efforts at stealth influence-peddling notwithstanding, in practice, the bureau sustained the NWCCR with technical support, publications, and even policy decisions. Bureau staff members fanned out to organize local and regional activities. Grassroots organizing stimulated the formation of state and local affiliates. The NWCCR and its affiliated bodies quickly circulated digests of the proposed civil rights bill provided by the Women's Bureau and initiated the "write for rights" campaign to support the administration's bill.[96] Members of Congress received a mountain of mail from the members of more than three hundred women's organizations as a result of the campaign. After the Johnson administration achieved passage of the Civil Rights Act of 1964, rather than disbanding the women's civil rights coalition moved to facilitate voluntary compliance with the public accommodations section of the new law in southern communities. For example, affiliated groups volunteered to escort black children into newly desegregated schools.

By 1964 the policy revolution in the passage of the 1963 Equal Pay Act and the 1964 Civil Rights Act and the nascent feminist activism within state commissions on the status of women put Johnson's appointee for Women's Bureau director, Mary Dublin Keyserling, in the curious position of administratively supporting institutions more inclined to promote equal rights feminism. (Peterson left the director job to become Johnson's special assistant for consumer affairs.) Jo Freeman wrote in 1975 that the women serving on the Equal Employment Opportunity Commission (EEOC), the President's Commission on the Status of Women, and state commissions were ideal candidates for cooptability "largely because their immersion into the facts of female status and the details of sex-discrimination cases made them very conscious of the need for change."[97] Even though Peterson failed to turn the Women's Bureau into the clerical worker for the women's movement, she left it still dependent on women's organizations for any success in policy formation. The next chapter explores how the Women's Bureau functioned more like a middle manager: it lost control over setting the political agenda of women's organizations but continued its central role in maintaining the communication networks that furthered the feminist cause.

CHAPTER 4

Backstage Activism

Feminist Organizing Under
Mary Dublin Keyserling, 1964-1968

"I DON'T KNOW where all those frustrated women are that Betty Friedan is talking about," stated Mary Dublin Keyserling, the Women's Bureau's fourth director, on one of her frequent visits to women's groups
in 1964.[1] *The Feminine Mystique,* published the same year the PCSW
presented its report to President Kennedy, could not have been more
dissimilar. To Friedan, cultural prescriptions that a woman's only
legitimate vocation was wife and mother caused the suburban house-
wife's ennui; she attacked Margaret Mead, who wrote the foreword to
the PCSW's report, *American Women,* as one of the architects of this
"feminine mystique." *American Women* avoided an analysis of the
ideological roots of women's oppression, focusing instead on specific
policy recommendations designed to create opportunities for working
women. Despite these analytical differences, both books publicized
women's second-class status to an increasingly receptive audience,
and both Keyserling and Friedan struggled—albeit in different ways—
to position the federal government behind gender equality. By the
mid-1960s, Women's Bureau-sponsored committees, conferences,
and War on Poverty projects attracted larger numbers of women into
systematic study of the causes of inequality and offered forums for
expression of discontent with the slow pace of equal opportunity
enforcement by federal and state governments. Keyserling nonetheless
underestimated the mounting frustration of women working within
government-sponsored communications networks, and, as a result,
failed to anticipate their impatience with the Women's Bureau's reluctance to embrace wholly equal rights feminism.

This chapter documents how the Women's Bureau's efforts to
create and sustain state commissions on the status of women led to
the unintended consequence of providing forums for the emergence

of a feminist critique of the absence of gender equality provisions in state and federal policies. The Women's Bureau brought together women who eventually attacked its role in convincing the Equal Employment Opportunity Commission to rule that protective labor laws did not violate Title VII of the 1964 Civil Rights Act barring discrimination in employment. The resulting "crisis" over the best way to represent women's interests convinced many feminist activists working within government that insider tactics alone would not lead to the meaningful social change they came to expect.[2]

With the passage of equal opportunity laws, the Women's Bureau's policies became even more contradictory and inconsistent. Within government, male bureaucrats' unwillingness to take women's concerns seriously sometimes caused the Women's Bureau to function as an aggressive proponent of equal opportunity. The bureau promoted state commissions on the status of women which also pressed for women's rights. Even so, it remained committed to protective labor legislation and continued to oppose the Equal Rights Amendment. Dorothy Haener explains how this incongruity provoked independent action by women working on government policy: "She [Dollie Lowther Robinson] talked of the U.S. Women's Bureau saying one thing and then instructing her to go up on Capitol Hill in Washington and talk to the congressmen about doing the other thing. That's the way it was behind the scenes all the time. You knew nothing was going to happen unless you had a pressure group that was going to be pressuring."[3] Nothing alienated activists more than the Women's Bureau's work behind the scenes to pressure the EEOC to rule that protective labor legislation did not violate the intent of Title VII. Missed opportunities to recruit additional policy partners within the emerging women's movement left the Women's Bureau vulnerable to programmatic integration within the Labor Department and stigmatized it as an antifeminist force.

Social movement feminists and, later, historians failed to realize that the Women's Bureau's activities remained inexorably connected to the reform impulses in the Kennedy and Johnson administrations that favored technocratic solutions to social problems instead of ideological ones.[4] The Council of Economic Advisors, employees in the Labor Department, and other analysts remaining from the Kennedy administration provided continuity from one Democratic administration to the next, maintaining the position that full employment would eliminate inequality by creating opportunities and eliminating competition for jobs. Federal employment policies, which included promoting minimum wage and maximum hours legislation to increase the purchasing power of the working poor, became state policies by the mid-1960s because of the Women's Bureau's influence over the deliberations and recommendations of state commissions on the status of women. This stake that the Women's Bureau had in state legislation to further Johnson's economic policies explains its reluctance to abandon anachronistic protective labor laws.

Mary Dublin Keyserling, described by Undersecretary of Labor John Henning as "a technician with a strong sense of social responsibility," had little in common with social movement feminists like Betty Friedan.[5] A Barnard graduate with all but the dissertation for a Ph.D. in economics from the London School of Economics and Columbia University, Keyserling entered government service as Eleanor Roosevelt's adviser on women's issues with the Office of Civilian Defense during World War II and in the postwar years worked in the Office of International Trade in the Department of Commerce. Out of place in the Eisenhower administration, she left government to influence policy from the private sector, forming a think tank of Keynesian economists with her husband Leon Keyserling, a former member of President Truman's Council of Economic Advisors. At their Council on Economic Progress, Mary Keyserling published *Poverty and Deprivation in the United States,* which argued that a growth economy, guaranteed by federal support of a strong union movement and social welfare measures such as minimum wage and unemployment insurance, would solve social problems by putting people to work.[6] Keyserling's reputation as an economic reformer, although earning her a place on the PCSW's Committee on Protective Legislation and a role in the Great Society, unsettled Republican senators John Tower of Texas and Milward W. Simpson of Wyoming, who voted against her confirmation as Women's Bureau director on April 10, 1964, because of her affiliation with "left-wing and pro-Communist groups."[7]

Back in government with the Women's Bureau, Keyserling actively promoted Johnson's domestic programs, calling the War on Poverty "one of the most significant undertakings in the history of the American presidency" and comparing the Great Society to Franklin D. Roosevelt's New Deal.[8] On the stump for Johnson in the 1964 presidential campaign before women's groups in particular, she credited the Kennedy and Johnson administrations for "improving the status of women more than in any other period since women won the right to vote in 1920."[9] In fact, the Democratic National Committee's pamphlet for the campaign, "Women in the USA: Partners in Peace, Achievement and Opportunities," embraced the Women's Bureau's policy victories in the 1960s as historic steps toward full equality.[10] On the other hand, in castigating Senator Barry M. Goldwater, the Republican candidate for president in 1964, for voting against measures to increase purchasing power proposed by the Kennedy and Johnson administrations—tax reduction, increases in unemployment compensation, the Area Redevelopment Act, and the youth employment bill—Keyserling raised the specter of the three recessions and high unemployment rate that had occurred during the Eisenhower administration.[11]

By defining the causes and outcomes of discrimination against women, not as violations of the principle of equal rights but as a waste of human resources, the recommendations of the President's Commission on the Status of Women empowered the Women's Bureau to advocate that War on Poverty programs include the employment and training needs of women and girls. Moreover, attention to women as an untapped resource seemed appropriate since one-fifth of female college graduates worked either as factory operatives or as sales, clerical, or service workers.[12] With the passage of the Employment Opportunities Act of 1964, the Labor Department became the federal government's primary administrator of youth employment and manpower training programs. Part A of Title I of the act created the Job Corps, modeled after the New Deal's Civilian Conservation Corps, and Part B founded the Neighborhood Youth Corps (NYC).[13] The Women's Bureau released several publications directing women and girls to these training programs for higher-paying jobs in the trades and crafts. Pamphlets written for high school- and college-age women advertised the NYC and federally funded loan and scholarship programs. Other publications targeting women already in the labor force described on-the-job training and apprenticeship opportunities offered by the Labor Department's Office of Manpower, Automation, and Training (OMAT).[14]

Labor Department projects focusing on women replicated the coalition politics characteristic of the regional employment conferences and the deliberations of the PCSW instituted by Esther Peterson in the Kennedy administration. OMAT-supported state-by-state workshops to aid women's organizations in the implementation of the education and training recommendations of the PCSW, including efforts to ensure that regional federal offices and state agencies avoided counseling girls to consider only a few sex-typed jobs or to rush into marriage without acquiring vocational skills.[15] Similarly, OMAT awarded the American Association of University Women a grant to fund an eight-week seminar for employment services officials to refine techniques on counseling mature women reentering the labor market. This project received a hearty endorsement from Keyserling, who reminded Howard Rosen, assistant director of OMAT, that women with college degrees "are not utilizing their full potential because of the almost total lack of specialized vocational training."[16] When the Los Angeles YWCA did not receive federal funds on the grounds that its proposal for a life skills program for Mexican American women lacked representation from that group, some nudging behind the scenes by the Women's Bureau forged a compromise that released funds for the program on the condition that a Mexican American woman direct the project.[17] The National Council of Catholic Women, the YWCA, the National Council of Jewish Women, and Church Women United also qualified for government work-training grants.

President Johnson turned to this coalition for support of his War on Poverty initiatives. When President Kennedy sought organizational support for his civil rights policies, the Women's Bureau organized a women's conference that culminated in the formation of an advisory committee, the National Women's Committee on Civil Rights. In the same vein, a national women's conference on the War on Poverty led to the creation of a Women's Advisory Council on Poverty comprised of representatives from the Women's Bureau's traditional organizational partners. Johnson hoped that the Council would mobilized public support for his programs. This same coalition made up the membership of the Women in Community Service (WICS) to support training programs for women and girls under the Job Corps.[18]

The Women's Bureau's administration of state commissions on the status of women also maintained coalition politics. Any group organizing a campaign for a state commission received from Washington model executive orders and budgets, instructions on how to write press releases, suggested agendas for inaugural meetings, and sample organizational charts. Once a governor or a legislature established a commission, Keyserling wrote a thank-you letter offering services from the bureau's nearest regional office.[19] Regional representatives worked almost exclusively on the organization and deliberations of these commissions, often attending organizing sessions and subsequent meetings to give technical advice. The Women's Bureau facilitated the process by which, as Jo Freeman argues, state commissions contributed to the formation of a mass-based women's movement: agitation for commissions brought women "who otherwise would not have worked together around matters of direct concern to women"; commission investigations convinced women that something should be done; and "the reports created a climate of expectations that something would be done."[20]

When Maryland's Democratic governor J. Millard Tawes refused to establish a commission, the American Association of University Women's Maryland chapter turned to female state legislators and the Women's Bureau for help. Regional representative Elsie Denison worked closely with the Maryland contingent of elected officials and representatives from state branches of the General Federation of Women's Clubs, the American Association of University Women, and the Maryland Federation of Business and Professional Women's Clubs to prepare a proposal for Tawes, who left office without forming a commission.[21] In 1965 this coalition succeeded in pressuring the next governor, Republican Spiro T. Agnew, to form one. The Maryland Commission on the Status of Women met for the first time in the Women's Bureau's offices for a briefing on the activities of working commissions.

In President Johnson's home state of Texas, Keyserling relied on both insider tactics and grassroots organizing to convince Democratic governor John Connally to form a state commission. A new Dallas field office and Keyserling's appearances in the state helped rally women's groups. Both Peterson and Keyserling went to Dallas for a reception introducing field representative Rhobia Taylor to the Texas women's community in 1964. Taylor, a Texas native and an overachieving club woman with memberships in the Business and Professional Women's Clubs, the American Association of University Women, and the National League for Nursing, promised to be an effective organizer.[22] When Keyserling returned to Dallas in January 1965 at the invitation of the Association of Women Students of Southern Methodist University, she reminded her audience that thirty-six states were working with the federal government to implement the recommendations in *American Women* without the help of the State of Texas.[23] In Houston, she appeared before sixteen hundred women attending an interfaith workshop arguing that a state commission "could replace outmoded ideas and abate prejudice against women as productive workers."[24] Back in Washington after the Houston visit, Keyserling called on the White House to arrange a meeting with Connally. After Connally conceded to political pressure and formed a commission in February 1965, Elizabeth Carpenter, President Johnson's top female adviser, received a list of twenty-five potential members from the Women's Bureau.[25]

The Women's Bureau sought labor union representation on commissions in particular. Because too many of the commissions had failed to involve significant numbers of labor union women, the Women's Bureau sponsored a conference for trade union professionals (vice presidents of national unions, education and research directors, local union presidents, and officers of women's departments or auxiliaries) to recruit members for commissions in the formative stages. Agnes Douty, chief of the Field Division, hoped to convince attendees to embark upon cooperative relationships to facilitate community action plans congruent with the public jobs and training programs in the Labor Department "to develop in communities needed services for working mothers such as day care centers, expansion of welfare services, and more training programs under private and public auspices."[26] One of the most tireless commission organizers, the director for the midwestern region Marguerite Gilmore, shared Esther Peterson's trade union and New Dealer allegiances. Like Peterson, Gilmore became involved with trade unionism through summer schools for women workers in the 1930s. After pursuing graduate training in economics at the University of Chicago for a year, she joined Franklin D. Roosevelt's New Deal as director of the Illinois Workers Education Program for the Works Progress Administration (WPA) and remained in government during World War II with stints on the War Labor Board and the Wage Stabilization Board. Between Democratic administrations in the 1950s, Gilmore served as metropolitan director for the Chicago YWCA.[27]

The fact that the pro-ERA, career woman–oriented BPW took the lead in organizing state commissions and tended to dominate commission memberships probably motivated Bureau staffers to interest labor union women in the commission movement. Nineteen BPW state branches made establishing a commission a primary goal as early as 1963.[28] In Michigan, the first state to have a status of women commission, BPW members composed one-third of the membership.[29] Eight Kentucky Federation members served on their state's commission because of the political clout of former national BPW president and former member of the PCSW's Civil and Political Status Committee, Katherine Peden, who, as the first female commerce commissioner for the State of Kentucky, convinced Democratic governor Edward T. Breathitt to sign an executive order in 1963 establishing a commission to be administered by her office.[30] Significantly, BPW members chaired one-third of the forty-five commissions formed by 1966.[31]

The interest group politics of midwestern Democratic governors in Illinois, Wisconsin, Minnesota, and Indiana helped Gilmore's cause to seek diverse commission memberships. The Wisconsin Commission on the Status of Women formed by Governor John W. Reynolds included four members from labor unions along with active presidents of state and local branches of the American Association of University Women, the General Federation of Women's Clubs, the National Council of Catholic Women, and the BPW.[32] In Indiana, Roger D. Branigan appointed Florence Murray, an inspector with the state labor department's Bureau of Women and Children, to his commission along with commission members representing the AFL-CIO and the League of Women Voters.[33] Illinois governor Otto Kerner appointed Addie Wyatt of Chicago, program director of District I, United Packinghouse Workers Union of America and a former member of the Protective Labor Legislation Subcommittee of the PCSW, as one of the ten community representatives to the state commission. Harriet Wolf, superintendent of the Women's and Children's Division of the Illinois Department of Labor, and Mary Lou Koonce, president of the Illinois Business and Professional Women's Clubs, joined Wyatt as commission members.[34]

The Minnesota Commission on the Status of Women had a similar composition, and its mission supported PCSW goals. Governor Karl Rolvaag's executive order charged forty-five Minnesotans to construct state policies paralleling the federal government's policy revolution: "It is clear from the Presidential Commission's report that state action is necessary to remove prejudices, customs, and laws that prevent women from participating as full citizens."[35] Rolvaag appointed former PCSW member and former president of the National Council of Jewish Women Viola Hymes chairman. Hymes described herself and the other appointees to the Minnesota Commission on the Status of Women as "just us housewives," but those housewives represented a Who's Who of political activism in the state: an executive director of a local YWCA, a past president of the Minnesota section of the National Council of Jewish Women, a president of the United Church Women, five representatives from labor unions, and a past president of the Minnesota Federation of Business and Professional Women's Clubs.[36] Committees on employment opportunities, civil and political rights, education, and home and community service expanded the coalition even further.[37]

Regional conferences and public hearings involved women throughout Minnesota in dialogues about their economic and civic and political status. A regional conference held in Duluth, cosponsored by the Women's Bureau and the state labor department, focused on employment placement in the economically depressed region. Organizing in Duluth generated action plans to educate high school and vocational counselors about the employment needs of young women. To inform the public on the importance of a state equal pay law, the commission's Employment Opportunities Committee arranged several "town meetings" with representatives from state branches of national women's organizations, business groups, and labor unions.[38] For its part, the Civil and Political Status Committee used hearings and conferences to publicly oppose a state statute that allowed women to request exemption from jury duty solely on the grounds that their responsibilities for the home precluded any extended commitment to civic duty. Relying on the PCSW's rejection of the argument that women as a group should be excused of rights and responsibilities as citizens, the committee endorsed a repeal of the exemption.[39]

Such public attention to the status of women inspired Jo Ann Louma from the rural village of Babbitt, Minnesota, to write to the Women's Bureau for advice on how to address discrimination against female teachers with children by the local school board. The reply signed by Keyserling directed her to the Minnesota Commission on the Status of Women for assistance.[40] The women's rights neophyte from Babbitt then sent a handwritten letter to Viola Hymes declaring that she and her friends had agreed that a resolution passed by the Babbitt School Board not to hire any female teachers with school-age children must be discriminatory. In her capacity as commission chairman, Hymes sent a telegram to the Babbitt School Board protesting the action: "We believe that this policy discriminates against many able women with children below college level age who are well able to make satisfactory arrangements for the care of those children while their mothers are at work. The Governor's Commission urges you to reevaluate this position."[41] Deciding not to rely solely on moral persuasion, though, the commission's administrative assistant, Mary Lou Hill, asked the Civil and Political Rights and Employment Opportunities Committees to get involved, and she also notified the Minnesota Teachers Association, the American Civil Liberties Union, and the state Board of Education of the discriminatory practice.[42]

The investigations of the Minnesota commission's Employment Opportunities Committee sometimes led to feminist action that co-opted the Women's Bureau's tolerance of gender difference policies. When evaluations of labor union contracts revealed sex discrimination in seniority clauses and pay scales, unions requested that the committee discern female industrial workers' attitudes toward the state's maximum hours law. Subsequent surveys revealed a consensus that such a law proved detrimental to promotion, hiring, and training of female workers, a finding that could not be ignored. Sex-segregated help wanted ads also drew the attention of the committee. With the support of the full commission, the committee sent a letter to publishers of Minnesota newspapers objecting to separate want ads by gender. Abandoning such a practice, the letter suggested, "would have the added advantage of removing psychological road blocks for persons of both sexes wishing to make full use of their abilities without regard to whether abilities are 'masculine' or 'feminine.'"[43]

Flashes of independence on the Minnesota commission did not deter the Women's Bureau from trying to direct its policies. A misunderstanding regarding a newspaper article in the *Minneapolis Star Tribune* on the President's Commission on the Status of Women illustrates how closely the bureau monitored developments in Minnesota. *Tribune* staff reporter Judy Vick wrote an article suggesting that the PCSW had recommended passage of the Equal Rights Amendment. Within days of publication of Vick's article, Viola Hymes received a note from Keyserling seeking an explanation: "This was more than a little disturbing to us as I am sure it was to you. Perhaps some day you can find a way to call attention to this error. I am sure it couldn't have appeared in the report of the Civil and Political Status Committee."[44] Armed with a copy of *American Women,* Hymes visited the *Tribune* offices to meet with Vick and the women's editor. Rather than print a correction, the two journalists accepted Hymes's suggestion to publish another article reviewing Pauli Murray's proposal for the PCSW's Political and Civil Status Committee that women pursue equal rights in the courts applying the Fourteenth Amendment.[45]

Accelerated activism in other states and the development of a national state commission network incited a disparate group of Ohio women's organizations to unite under a single political goal, the formation of a state commission on the status of women. State BPW president Ellen Holstrup was convinced that Ohio's Republican governor, James A. Rhodes, refused to establish a commission because he did not want to pursue a policy initiated by liberal Democrat John F. Kennedy.[46] In response to Rhodes's repeated refusals to convene a commission on women's status, the Public Affairs Committee of the Ohio YWCA organized a meeting of women's organizations' leaders for the purpose of building a statewide coalition. Regional representative Marguerite Gilmore attended with representatives from the NCJW, the LWV, the Ohio Council of Catholic Women, the BPW, the AAUW, the National Council of Negro Women, and the YWCA. She gave a progress report on the work of existing state commissions before the participants set about forming the Ad Hoc Steering Committee on the Status of Women.[47] Representatives from the AAUW and the BPW, already busy with internal commission action committees, left a power vacuum on the newly formed state steering committee to be filled by women from less politically active organizations. Helen Samuels, a member of the Metropolitan Columbus League of Women Voters, served as a liaison between the Ad Hoc Committee and state and local leagues.[48] Dorothy Langley, of the Columbus branch of the National Council of Catholic Women, became Ad Hoc Committee chairman, and Mrs. Henry Grinsfelder, representing the Columbus section of the NCJW, was elected secretary.[49]

Extensive media coverage of the Ad Hoc Committee on the Status of Women's invitation to 250 leaders of women's organizations to participate in organizing a citizens' committee on the status of women compelled Rhodes to abandon his commitment not to create additional government commissions, committees, or agencies. Twenty-four hours before the organizational meeting, Rhodes announced the formation of a governor's committee on the status of women to present a report to him in a year's time.[50] Statewide press coverage of women's rights activism had triggered Rhodes's interest in avoiding controversial issues.[51] Yet, his concession to the commission movement did not deter forty-one women's organizations from creating the Ohio Citizens' Committee on the Status of Women.[52] The governor's promise, evincing political clout, emboldened the coalition to continue the campaign for a permanent commission.

Nevertheless, the Governor's Committee on the Status of Women marked a victory for the commission movement, as members of the Women's Bureau coalition moved on to a policymaking body in state government and represented Ohio in national commission institutions. Representatives from the National Council of Catholic Women, the YWCA, the National Council of Jewish Women, the AAUW, and United Church Women acquired seats on the twenty-six-member committee. Close to a fourth of the membership—six appointees— came from the Ohio Federation of Business and Professional Women's Clubs, including Rhodes's appointee for chairman Olive Huston, Republican mayor of Xenia, Ohio. To be sure, BPW leadership of the initial lobbying effort for a status commission paid off in committee representation, but its Republican ties did not hurt either. Notably, Rhodes did not appoint any representatives from black women's organizations.[53]

Research subcommittees revealed persistent discrimination against women workers in promotions, in entrance to the professions, in training and education, and in wage rates. Following the PCSW's practice of inviting professionals to serve as consultants to subcommittees, several female professionals from business, academia, and government embarked on research projects at the behest of the committee, thereby expanding the reach of the commission movement beyond core women's organizations. Members of women's organizations became investigators, too. For example, the Columbus, Ohio, section of the National Council of Jewish Women urged its members to read the Ohio General Assembly's report on discriminatory labor laws in order to make informed contributions to committee deliberations.[54] Researchers on the Counseling and Education Subcommittee discovered high school classes on certain subjects not open to girls, and investigations of women's status in higher education produced evidence of female enrollment quotas and inequities in scholarship awards.[55] The Opportunities Subcommittee put an exclamation point on the significance of educational discrimination by publicizing the dearth of women in Ohio's professional ranks, where women comprised less than 3 percent of attorneys, 6 percent of physicians, and less than 1 percent of scientists and engineers.[56]

The Employment Practices Subcommittee deviated from the Women's Bureau's program by reporting that protective labor legislation in Ohio "shut women out of quite a number of jobs" and revealing how employers used female difference to justify keeping women out of supervisory and managerial positions.[57] Survey data documented that one-fourth of employers in private industry would lay off women first, and close to half of employers relied on the difference argument to explain why they would not promote women to supervisory positions—they were "emotionally unstable," "lacked skills or showed an unwillingness to be trained," or had "physical limitations."[58] More than 50 percent of employers in the service industry reported that female workers were "generally undependable."[59] A similar bias against female workers surfaced in a survey of the education field, where 75 percent of school districts reported policies that prohibited the promotion of women to administrative positions because of "emotional instability and the need to recruit more men to the field."[60]

By advocating public policies to address documented economic and educational inequities between men and women, the final report of the Governor's Committee, *Women in the Wonderful World of Ohio*, had more in common with the Great Society than Ohio's Republican politics. The report's title, taken from a travelogue published by the Department of Tourism entitled *The Wonderful World of Ohio*, must have seemed ludicrous given the report's documentation of persistent inequality.[61] In spite of Rhodes's penchant for bureaucratic retrenchment—he organized a group of business leaders to suggest governmental reorganization in much the same way Eisenhower did in reorganizing the Department of Labor in the 1950s—recommendations suggested the formation of several new state committees, divisions, and programs: a consumer protection bureaucracy, a child care services program, a committee to interpret the impact of Title VII on employment in Ohio, a state committee to set standards for household employment, and a women's division within the Bureau of Employment Services. Additional recommendations urged Rhodes to appoint more women to existing policy-making committees, boards, and offices in state government.[62]

Women's Bureau officials actively encouraged state commissions to expand governmental authority through the passage of state labor legislation and the creation of employment programs. Alice Morrison monitored closely the deliberations of the Maryland commission's Committee on Employment and Labor Standards. Both Morrison and regional representative Elsie Denison attended committee meetings as "resource persons."[63] During the first meeting, Denison commented on possible improvements to Maryland's labor laws. Indeed, subsequent recommendations included strengthening the labor department and the passage of a state equal pay law.[64] In South Carolina, Keyserling won praise from Olive Furth, president of the Conference of the Status of Women, for pointing out potential goals, including state labor legislation, at the first meeting "without antagonizing anyone."[65] By 1966, state commissions in Oklahoma, North Dakota, Indiana, and Utah had secured the passage of both minimum wage and equal pay laws and West Virginia gained an equal pay law. Moreover, commission activism in South Dakota, Maine, and Illinois led to the creation of additional state programs for training and employment placement. Commissions in Indiana, Iowa, Nebraska, Pennsylvania, Rhode Island, and Oregon held statewide conferences cosponsored by the state labor department and the Women's Bureau to generate interest and activism for labor legislation and training programs.[66]

The regional representative for the southeastern states, Dianne McKaig, a Harvard-trained attorney specializing in labor law, failed to convince the North Carolina commission to try to achieve equity while standing pat on protective labor laws. The commission petitioned the North Carolina General Assembly for an amendment to the minimum wage law expanding coverage to include men working in certain occupations. Another recommendation sought equity through new legislation "prohibiting wage, salary or hours discrimination on the basis of sex" and requiring equal pay for equal work.[67] Such actions met with McKaig's approval, but she tried to protect an existing maximum hours law for women only when a businessman on the committee suggested revising entirely the state's maximum hours laws instead of introducing an amendment to include men.[68] Lacking a consensus on the issue, the commission did not add amendments to maximum hours laws to its legislative program.

Lest the state commissions consider renegade recommendations such as supporting the Equal Rights Amendment or weakening protective labor laws, the Women's Bureau tried to keep commissions in line through communications networks created by the regional representative system and national conferences. Agnes Douty's memo to her field-workers reveals a deliberate plan to determine final commission recommendations: "A number of GCSW's will soon be ready to report to their governors. It strikes me as a very important opportunity for the regional directors to be involved in the thinking on the context of these proposals before they are sent on to the governors. This would prevent unwise recommendations based on lack of adequate understanding of an issue. Such proposals might be caught before they go to the governors, even on an interim basis."[69]

The first national status commission conference in 1964 enabled the Women's Bureau to ensure that its constituents, to borrow Douty's euphemistic language, had an "adequate understanding" of the issues and avoided "unwise recommendations." The formal program, dominated by state and federal labor officials, stayed on the message of the importance of labor laws. Ten

Minnesotans paid their own expenses to Washington to hear Secretary of Labor Willard Wirtz and other federal bureaucrats outline the Johnson administration's War on Poverty and full employment goals. In summarizing the work of the 1964 national conference, Keyserling brought economic policy priorities to the table again by linking stronger minimum wage laws with increased purchasing power: "Stronger minimum wages is one of the truly exciting developments coming out of the work of our commissions. You are recognizing that we must move all disadvantaged people forward together."[70] The organ of the BPW, the *National Business Woman*, reported that after Keyserling spoke, someone from the audience said "Let's make it unfashionable for women to feel frustrated."[71] Similar expressions of rising consciousness surfaced informally when commission representatives had time to talk with one another. The numbers of women who complained that their work on commissions "often made them laughing stocks in the stories devoted to their efforts" impressed Wisconsin's commission chairman, Kathryn Clarenbach.[72]

Keyserling, unmoved by the stirrings of discontent, used her power within the Labor Department to influence EEOC rulings on the relationship of state laws to Title VII. Labor union activist Dorothy Haener, one of the founders of the National Organization for Women, believed that Keyserling "was just absolutely deaf to anyone who suggested that state protective laws didn't protect, that they did discriminate sometimes."[73] Months before President Johnson appointed commissioners to the EEOC, charged to administer Title VII as of July 1965, a small, all-female subcommittee of the ICSW convened to make recommendations for investigating sex discrimination to the full committee. Esther Peterson wrote to Keyserling, a subcommittee member, offering the data collection services of the Labor Department's bureaus and divisions to bring facts to bear on the state labor laws question before any rush to judgment by the EEOC. The two labor officials in the group, Keyserling and Carol Cox from the Labor Department's Solicitor's Office, saw no conflict between the intent of Title VII and sex-based labor laws. Mary Eastwood representing the Justice Department and Evelyn Harrison from the Civil Service Commission disagreed and wanted the ICSW to interpret Title VII as overriding discriminatory state laws. The deadlock produced two reports to the full committee.[74] Because the Labor Department controlled the ICSW, the final recommendation to Franklin D. Roosevelt Jr., chairman of the EEOC, deferred to the regulatory flexibility recommended by the President's Commission on the Status of Women in urging the EEOC not to suggest that state legislatures invalidate existing laws until they could be amended to extend similar protections to men.[75] Consequently, the commissioners ruled that the choice between protection and equity could be avoided "if these protective laws were amended to provide for *greater flexibility* [emphasis added]," which the PCSW's Protective Labor Legislation Committee had proposed in 1963.[76]

A conference held in July 1965 for state commission chairmen gave the Women's Bureau the opportunity to suggest policies to end discrimination based on sex without repealing state labor laws. Women's Bureau staff encouraged commission members in each state to evaluate progress on achieving equity in a national context. Women attending the workshop on "The Legal Status of Women" received handouts outlining ways to address discrimination in family and property law. In the workshop on "Title VII and State Law," Bureau staffers hoped to avoid the state labor laws issue by convincing commission activists to work toward amending state fair employment practices laws to include sex: "Does your state have a Fair Employment Practices law? If so, does it include sex? If not, should action be taken to include prohibition of sex discrimination?"[77]

There is no doubt the Women's Bureau welcomed Title VII's prohibition of sex discrimination despite aggressive advocacy against repeal of existing state protective labor laws. Keyserling interpreted Title VII as congressional recognition of the importance of women's skills to economic growth.[78] A detailed procedural guideline on Title VII enforcement for the EEOC produced in the Women's Bureau reminded inspectors that they must investigate instances of discriminatory employment practices against female workers. The section on state labor laws was surprisingly evenhanded—inspectors should not allow state labor laws to override Title VII without question but instead embark on thorough investigations into possible use of those laws to justify sex discrimination. Moreover, Keyserling wanted the EEOC to reject the idea that Congress intended to limit Title VII enforcement of equal pay to the occupations covered in the Equal

Pay Act.[79] To help enforcement along, the Women's Bureau in 1965 carefully compiled letters to the Labor Department from women seeking information about or redress under Title VII for the EEOC to consider.[80]

The Citizens' Advisory Council on the Status of Women (CACSW) produced a separate report to the EEOC, supported by the Labor Department, arguing for a narrow interpretation of Section 703(e) of Title VII allowing employers to hire on the basis of sex—bona fide occupational qualification (BFOQ)—"if a qualification is reasonably necessary to the normal operation of that particular business or enterprise."[81] Section 703(e) opened the door to employer maintenance of men's and women's jobs, a loophole opposed by Keyserling and the CACSW. Johnson's appointee to chair the CACSW, former PCSW member and former BPW national president Margaret Hickey, supervised the development of a policy paper on the implications of Title VII of the 1964 Civil Rights Act for female workers. Months before the CACSW released its report, Keyserling urged Secretary Wirtz to push for a restrictive interpretation of the BFOQ.[82] The CACSW agreed, arguing that because men and women are equally qualified to perform well in most jobs the EEOC should instead focus on specifying ways Section 703(e) cannot be applied to exclude women from employment.[83] Additionally, its report to the EEOC mentioned explicitly media treatment of the sex provision that ridiculed or made light of the existence of discrimination against women and suggested that the EEOC begin immediately to inform the public on the importance of the law in solving unemployment among women, particularly black women.

The CACSW supported position papers with deliberate feminist action using government communication networks. A year before the formation of the National Organization for Women, the CACSW contributed to making sex-segregated want ads a political issue by circulating, to all of the state status of women commissions, the BPW's Washington, D.C., chapter's resolution condemning the EEOC's inaction in declaring separate want ads a violation of Title VII.[84] After Hickey resigned her chairmanship in 1966, President Johnson replaced her with Senator Maurine Neuberger, who presided over an expanded staff dedicated to updating the PCSW's recommendations. Under Neuberger's chairmanship, the

CACSW's Family Law and Policy Task Force, which included avowed feminists and PCSW veterans Alice Rossi, Marguerite Rawalt, and Mary Eastwood, considered the controversial topic of reproductive freedom, promoting the notion that "the right of a woman to control her own body was a basic civil right."[85]

Women's rights advocates on both sides of the labor standards issue were equally indignant at the EEOC commissioners' cavalier treatment of the "sex" provision in Title VII. The activism generated by the PCSW inside and outside the federal government had little impact on the EEOC, as chairman Roosevelt chose men as his top aides, bureaucrats who were uncharacteristically brazen in publicly dismissing women's concerns. Just at the time the EEOC started deliberations on sex discrimination guidelines in August 1965, a *New York Times* article, "For Instance, Can She Pitch for the Mets?" noted that the deputy counsel to the EEOC, Richard K. Berg, brought up the "bunny question"— whether or not a Playboy Bunny would meet BFOQ—during a White House conference on equal opportunity. In a letter to the editor, Esther Peterson accused the *Times* and Berg with failing to come to terms with the seriousness of sex discrimination, and, in technocratic fashion, advocated "factual, unbiased treatment of the story of discrimination against the woman worker in man's world of work."[86] Pleas for judicious action on sex discrimination did not prevent the executive director of the EEOC, Herman Edelsberg, from denigrating the mandate to investigate the discrimination. At New York University's Annual Conference on Labor, Olya Margolin chastised Edelsberg for asserting that sex discrimination did not carry the same moral authority as racial discrimination.[87] Margolin urged Keyserling to ask the CACSW to take a similar public stand against the recalcitrant EEOC director.[88] Representative Martha Griffiths, Democrat from Michigan, went a step further and read several of Edelsberg's comments into the *Congressional Record,* including a statement he made at his first press conference that men were entitled to have female secretaries. "Are such men qualified professionally to enforce Title VII?" she asked her colleagues in the House.[89] To add legitimacy to the argument that the EEOC must be held accountable on gender, Griffiths referred to the CACSW's 1965 report and read every council member's name into the *Record.*

Until the formation of the National Organization for Women (NOW) in 1966, Women's Bureau employee Catherine East single-handedly ensured some national coordination of protofeminist activities emerging in response to the EEOC's deafness to women's complaints. East was transferred from the U.S. Civil Service Commission to work on one of the subcommittees of the PCSW, where she received "a liberal education in the pervasiveness of sex discrimination, not only throughout our social, legal, and economic systems, but in the total structure of our society."[90] She used her insider status to make the PCSW recommendations more potent. For example, in drafting the executive order establishing the Citizens' Advisory Council on the Status of Women, she made sure that its recommendations would be independent of the Labor Department and circulated to state commissions on the status of women. After the passage of the 1964 Civil Rights Act, East used her position as the staff officer on the Interdepartmental Committee on the Status of Women to funnel all the information she could get her hands on about any progress in improving the economic and civic status of women to a small group of activists in government Betty Friedan called "the Washington underground." Pauli Murray remembered that East could be found "toiling away in her tiny office at the U.S. Department of Labor, making frequent trips to the Xerox room to reproduce data for the packets she sent out to her small constituency."[91] East tried to convince Friedan to form an outside pressure group, a pattern of policy formation reminiscent of the Women's Bureau's advisory committees.

The Third Annual Conference for State Status of Women Commissions in June 1966 offered a more public forum for women to consider what to do about the EEOC. The conference format remained the same—workshops and panels facilitating dialogues among commission members and punctuated by keynote addresses by labor officials. However, the standard informational sessions characteristic of Women's Bureau–sponsored conferences failed to contain critics of the EEOC, especially after the first day's luncheon speaker, Martha Griffiths, circulated reprints of her speech on the floor of Congress reproaching Edelsberg.[92] Many delegates wanted to follow Griffiths's example. Kathryn Clarenbach used the opportunity to propose an action unanticipated by the Women's Bureau, a resolution denouncing the EEOC's inaction on sex discrimination.

Representatives from the National Woman's Party offered another resolution supporting the Equal Rights Amendment. Peterson and Keyserling ruled the resolutions from the floor out of order at a conference serving as a clearinghouse of information on state activities.[93] Officials representing the Johnson administration could not sanction an attack on the federal government. Thus, the labor officials rejected Clarenbach's idea to use the existing state commission structure to formally censure the EEOC and sustain pressure on the federal government to enforce gender equity.

The very public silencing of disillusioned state commission representatives precipitated a "crisis" that convinced Washington's feminist underground that the EEOC would not move on sex discrimination without being lobbied from a group independent of the federal government. Unbeknownst to Peterson and Keyserling, the night before the resolutions debacle Friedan invited Clarenbach to join a group assembled in her hotel room to discuss the ouster of Richard Graham from the EEOC. That evening Clarenbach convinced the group to utilize the existing mechanisms of the state commissions rather than creating a separate, competing organization. When Peterson and Keyserling refused to allow a resolution that the state commissions address EEOC policies because "government commissions cannot take action against other departments," they lost a loyal ally—Clarenbach gave up on insider tactics.[94] While Republican congresswomen Frances Bolton and Chase Going Woodhouse encouraged women to consider political activism, a small group occupying two tables passed notes that set the framework for a new women's rights organization. Friedan described the tension in the room: "I wonder if Esther Peterson and the other Women's Bureau officials and Cabinet members who talked down to us at lunch knew that those two front tables, so rudely, agitatedly whispering to one another and passing around notes written on paper napkins, were under their very noses organizing NOW."[95]

Even though NOW members questioned the efficacy of insider tactics, they could not ignore institutions organizing women in all fifty states. Before dispersing from Washington, twenty-eight women drafted the mission of NOW: "These agreements came after a discussion of the ruling that government commissions cannot take action against other government departments. It was felt that this is the time for action in this field."[96] Clarenbach became temporary chairman, and former PCSW activists Caroline Ware and Pauli Murray joined the steering committee. A month later, Clarenbach suggested that the steering committee clarify that NOW did not have a relationship with the federally sponsored state commissions without attacking an important source of new members.[97]

At the same time, manpower, antipoverty, and antidiscrimination initiatives, in failing to include women, caused the Women's Bureau to become more action oriented than social movement feminists realized. A manpower research bulletin, *Unused Manpower: The Nation's Loss*, released in 1966, noted that full employment goals must consider that "housewives, mothers, and students would at some time be freed from the economic necessity of working and be able to turn their attention to other activities."[98] Keyserling cried foul in a memo to Stanley Ruttenberg of OMAT, citing statistics on women's labor force participation indicating that quit rates would remain small. In response to manpower reports for the president that had also ignored the economic problems of women, Keyserling wrote extensive memos to the Manpower Administration's Office of Manpower Evaluation and Research (OMER) head Curtis C. Allen documenting women's vital economic contributions. As a result of a relationship between the Women's Bureau's Jean Wells and Helen Wood from OMER, the 1967 Manpower Report included a chapter on the underutilization of women and the inclusion of recommendations for expanded child care services.[99]

Information disseminated from other areas in the Labor Department echoed manpower reports in suggesting that women did not need or want to work. Remarkably, Secretary Wirtz often referred to women as "secondary workers." In a press release issued on April 11, 1966, the Bureau of Labor Statistics attributed high unemployment rates among women to a lack of a commitment to permanent, full-time work. Its unemployment survey stated: "Married women are preponderantly secondary wage earners and generally have more latitude in their decisions about work."[100] Again, Keyserling combated bias with the facts, pointing out to Joseph Goldberg, director of the BLS, that most of the women in the labor force are primary earners in their families. Nevertheless, the stereotype persisted in a pending report on graduate study that blamed women for not taking advantage of opportunities open to them. Wells recommended instead that the report indicate that "much more needs to be done to foster optimum development of talented womanpower."[101]

Prevailing stereotypes of female workers as cakewinners rather than breadwinners slanted many antipoverty programs toward male unemployment. The President's Task Force on Manpower Conservation set aside funds for programs designed for young men screened by the Selective Service. Apprenticeship programs directed outreach efforts toward young men in urban areas, and Neighborhood Youth Corps programs earmarked resources for inner-city boys. More importantly, equal employment opportunity policies concerned race, not gender, even though Labor Secretary Wirtz chaired the very committee responsible for a federal response to women's issues, the Interdepartmental Committee on the Status of Women.

Similar stereotypes appeared in Assistant Secretary of Labor Daniel Patrick Moynihan's report on black families, known as the Moynihan Report, which blamed female-headed families as the cause of poverty, crime, and delinquency in black communities. Moynihan, part of a small team that crafted War on Poverty legislative proposals, believed that government employment placement programs should emphasize strengthening the position of men in the black family, a role undermined by chronic unemployment and the legacy of slavery. Well aware of the policy implications of an analysis that emphasized the importance of a male breadwinner earning a family wage, Keyserling continued to stress the need for public support for working women. Speaking at the Conference on the Negro Woman in the U.S.A. on November 11, 1965, she suggested that Moynihan's assumption that women's unemployment might be necessary to stabilize the black family and end poverty violated the full employment goals of Johnson's economic policies. Instead, female heads of households needed government-sponsored child care and educational programs in order to become part of the economic mainstream as taxpayers and consumers.[102]

In an effort to combat bias in policy formation, Bureau staff members attempted to join coordinating committees reviewing training and education programs and to influence the direction of research studies. On hand as Labor Department insiders, Women's Bureau staffers constantly reminded program administrators that the unemployment rate for young women aged sixteen to nineteen had increased at a higher rate compared to that for young men in the mid-1960s.[103] Deputy Director Mary Hilton served on an interdepartmental task force to oversee all vocational guidance activities. In one case, the politically powerful Peterson, as assistant secretary of labor, made sure that Stanley Ruttenberg placed Women's Bureau staffers on any committee developing training programs for women receiving Aid to Families with Dependent Children (AFDC) payments.[104] In spite of Peterson's intervention, Keyserling had to request a role in developing child care guidelines accompanying the work incentive program for AFDC mothers.[105] In 1967, Isabel Striedel successfully convinced T. A. Chittenden, administrator of the Wage, Hour, and Public Contracts Divisions, to compile statistics by sex on hiring practices by businesses with government contracts.[106]

Feminist advocacy within the Labor Department included suggestions to recognize gender bias and antidiscrimination policies in publications and regulations. Guides and manuals regarding employment practices regularly omitted the provision of the 1964 Civil Rights Act prohibiting discrimination on account of sex. A Labor Department guide to grievance procedures left out "sex" as a category of discrimination, as did a booklet produced for personnel directors. Materials provided for an AFL-CIO conference on equal employment opportunity considered race only.[107] A stream of Women's Bureau memos urged that such omissions be corrected. Keyserling reminded the director of the Bureau of Employment Security, Robert Goodwin, that manuals to regional employment offices should note that request orders for workers specifying sex would be in violation of Title VII of the Civil Rights Act.[108] In many instances, staffers gently suggested to administrators that the use of the male pronoun would not always be perceived by the public as "generic."[109] Esther Peterson expressed frustration that she and the Women's Bureau acted constantly as watchdogs: "It is with real regret that the Women's Bureau and I often find ourselves forced into the position of seeming feminists when we feel this attitude is so outmoded and certainly one that should not be needed in this Department."[110]

The Women's Bureau also had to fight for inclusion of women and girls in a Job Corps program included in the Employment

Opportunity Act of 1964. Sargent Shriver, special assistant to the president and chairman of the President's Task Force on the War on Poverty, remained ignorant of women's employment needs, telling Betty Friedan, "Why should I try to train a woman, who would rather be my wife and the mother of my children, to use a computer?"[111] Shriver and other policymakers on the President's Task Force on the War on Poverty wanted to limit the number of girls in the Job Corps program because they envisioned establishing rural camps for boys replicating the Civilian Conservation Corps of the 1930s. The Women's Bureau disputed this plan in working papers documenting the training needs of women and girls, and staffers Beatrice McConnell and Jean Wells established a working relationship with the task force in an attempt to change members' male bias. In spite of this effort, task force member Jeanne Noble publicly announced plans to limit the number of girls participating in the Job Corps program to a quota of less than one-third.[112] It is not clear if the lone female member of the poverty task force made the public declaration to marshal political support against excluding girls. In any event, the announcement inspired Keyserling and her staff to draft a letter for Secretary Wirtz's signature, as chairman of the ICSW, explaining to Sargent Shriver, "There are more girls than boys aged 16–21 out of school, out of work, and in poverty."[113]

Representative Edith Green campaigned against quotas on female participation in Job Corps programs with mixed results. Even though she successfully amended the Job Corps section of the Employment Opportunity Act without a quota on female participation, at the signing ceremony of the bill by President Johnson, Adam Yarmolinksi, an aide to Sargent Shriver, took her aside to say that a "firm decision has been made to restrict participation of girls in the Job Corps to a maximum of one-sixth."[114] Green told Keyserling: "I've been sold down the river."[115] In 1967, Green orchestrated amendments to the Employment Opportunity Act mandating that 23 percent of the participants in Job Corps programs be girls. The first Job Corps contract after the 1967 amendments provided for residential centers to accommodate 6,500 girls.[116]

Representative Green was not the only women's advocate sold down the river on the implementation of the Employment Opportunity Act. Despite Secretary Wirtz's order stipulating that all bureaus and divisions would execute policies on the formation of the

Neighborhood Youth Corps, Leo R. Werts of the Manpower Administration neglected to include the Women's Bureau in policy deliberations. McConnell protested and wanted activity analyses written in the Manpower Administration to reflect her bureau's expertise in developing programs and policies in connection to training young women.[117] The department's Solicitor's Office received a protest of a different sort. Keyserling complained to Deputy Associate Solicitor Albert D. Misler that proposed regulations to execute the Employment Opportunity Act used the pronoun "he" or "him": "As a means of emphasizing the intention that boys and girls have equal opportunity to participate in this program, we would suggest that in those instances the words 'him or her' or 'he or she' as the context requires be used."[118] She also had to remind Misler that the section of the regulations on nondiscrimination omitted the word "sex."

Advocacy for female appointments to War on Poverty planning groups represented another effort to end male bias in policy decisions. Keyserling complained to Wirtz about the exclusion of women in significant War on Poverty positions: "Jeanne Noble is being pushed far down the line in the administrative structure. There are no women, as far as we can find out, being appointed at the top decision-making level."[119] At Keyserling's insistence, the ICSW recommended to the president that supervisors be required to make semiannual progress reports on the hiring of women in their respective agencies.[120] Before resigning from the War on Poverty task force in 1967, Noble recommended that a woman be chosen as a Job Corps deputy director.[121] Esther Peterson, too, pressed Wirtz to evaluate internal hiring policies, especially to redress the gender imbalance in regional offices. Additionally, to encourage placement of women in powerful and visible positions, the Women's Bureau provided John Macy of the Civil Service Commission with the names of qualified women for Supreme Court justice and deputy attorney general.[122]

President Johnson's inconsistent commitment to appointing women to higher-level government posts frustrated women's organizations. The PCSW's study of the federal civil service revealed that half of requests for personnel to the Federal Civil Service specified men only and that 94 percent of positions in the higher grades specified men. When the Civil Service Commission accepted the PCSW's recommendation to end the practice of stipulating the sex of applicants, placement of larger numbers of women in government service became a possibility overnight. CACSW chair Margaret Hickey considered the "great woman hunt" within the federal government one of the PCSW's most significant accomplishments and appealed to her fellow BPW members to continue to identify qualified women.[123] These expectations intensified when Johnson appointed women to forty-two executive departments by January 1964. The BPW had already submitted a list of qualified women to Johnson compiled by state and local branches as part of its Womanpower Pool Talent Search initiative begun after the PCSW's recommendations on federal appointments—and expected more appointments to follow.[124] With the increased "politicalization" of female appointments, Johnson's neglect of the issue after 1964 ensured that it would become part of the political agenda of women's organizations, including the new action-oriented group, the National Organization for Women. NOW complained to Johnson about the lack of female representation in the federal government.[125]

At the same time, the 1963 Equal Pay Act and Title VII of the 1964 Civil Rights Act gave women's organizations alternative means of fighting sex discrimination to solely relying on insider tactics such as working for favorable federal appointments; NOW and the BPW shared an interest in pressing the EEOC to outlaw protective labor legislation. In 1966 national BPW president, Sarah Jane Cunningham, explained that her organization had entered a new era of "implementation and effectiveness"—antidiscrimination laws shifted the BPW's focus from lobbying to litigation.[126] Toward that end, the BPW retained a law firm for advice on effective ways to use Title VII to end sex discrimination. From 1967 until the Supreme Court ruled state protective labor laws unconstitutional in 1971, counsel to the BPW joined several cases challenging protective labor legislation as *amicus curiae*. NOW's legal committee, chaired by the intrepid Marguerite Rawalt, pursued a similar strategy, working for appeals in two Title VII cases involving protective labor legislation: *Bowe v. Colgate-Palmolive* and *Mengelkoch v. State of California*. Unlike the BPW, however, NOW supported legal action with direct action against the EEOC. Political pressure compelled the EEOC to hold hearings on sex-segregated want ads in May 1967. The following December,

NOW organized pickets of EEOC regional offices.[127] Court cases and mounting political pressure caused the EEOC to reverse its previous guidelines indicating no conflict between protective labor legislation and Title VII in 1969.

The transformation of feminist advocacy from insider tactics to social movement activism weakened the Women's Bureau. The BPW, a prominent policy partner, pursued an independent agenda to end sex discrimination, including renewed interest in the Equal Rights Amendment. Betty Friedan, the leader of the National Organization of Women, considered the Women's Bureau part of a government conspiracy to undermine feminism.[128] As a result, for the first time in the Women's Bureau's history it could not count on an organized coalition of interest groups to fight for program integrity. More important, a series of court rulings on Title VII invalidated the Women's Bureau's core policies. A Labor Department reorganization in 1967 abolished independent bureaus in favor of management by assistant secretaries, ending the era of a separate agency representing women's interests in the federal government. Consequently, the Women's Bureau became a cog in the Wage and Labor Standards Administration. Needless to say, Keyserling chafed at the loss of independence. She perceived a requirement that all correspondence be reviewed with WLSA policy goals in mind as meddling in the bureau's work with its client groups and opposed all plans to have members of her staff move to a planning unit within the WLSA.[129] In 1970, on the outside of another Republican administration with Richard M. Nixon's election as president in 1968, Keyserling again turned her attentions to policymaking in the private sector—this time in the employ of a policy partner, the National Council of Jewish Women, to develop child care policies. In the Nixon administration, the Women's Bureau entered a new policy era in active support of the Equal Rights Amendment and other feminist issues. However, its methods of work did not change, only the allies.

Conclusion

"Linking Government and the Grassroots"

THIS STUDY PUTS the Women's Bureau in its proper context as a federal bureaucracy, limited by statute to a reliance on research and publicity in policy formation and beholden to its client groups, Congress and the Labor Department. While the Women's Bureau's public presentation remained consistent over time because deviations from its stated mission could jeopardize funding as an autonomous agency, its backstage behavior in the use of resources changed to fit the exigencies of postwar society. Economic planning within the federal government, made possible by the Employment Act of 1946 and the Manpower Development and Training Act of 1962, altered the mission of the Labor Department and its bureaus and divisions. During the 1950s in particular, employment placement programs dominated the Labor Department's activities within a Republican administration that de-emphasized the federal government's regulatory role and accentuated a partnership with business. The Labor Department in the New Frontier and Great Society renewed commitments to the establishment of regulatory mechanisms and increased funding for government programs while maintaining the manpower focus of the Eisenhower administration. As a consequence, the Women's Bureau's promotion of protective labor legislation for female wage earners before World War II was increasingly recast into a program that stressed publicizing job opportunities and advocating higher wages.

Postwar programmatic goals complemented the orientation of several women's organizations—representing millions of women through national and state branches—and women in labor unions. In addition, state labor departments sought the Women's Bureau's help in maintaining state regulatory laws. Professionals working in state labor departments and women's organizations and women with staff positions in trade unions formed long-term relationships with the career bureaucrats on the Women's Bureau's staff. These professional networks sustained the women's economic agenda within disparate service, professional, and religious women's organizations and labor unions. By the 1960s, in the context of the federal activism of the New Frontier, President Kennedy's appointee to head the Women's Bureau, Esther Peterson, persuaded the administration to act upon the women's economic agenda. The subsequent policy revolution in the Kennedy administration, with the creation of the President's Commission on the Status of Women in 1961 and the passage of the 1963 Equal Pay Act, enabled the Women's Bureau to more aggressively and publicly represent women's interests both inside and outside of the federal government. Surprisingly, by the late 1960s, this effort had become so successful that additional state and federal agencies emerged to represent women's interests and new feminist organizations developed. In the ensuing social movements of the late 1960s and early 1970s, the Women's Bureau, which had successfully fought integration of its program during several reorganizations within the Labor Department since 1920, lost independence. Mary Dublin Keyserling's refusal to endorse the Equal Rights Amendment contributed to a breakdown of the public support necessary to defend the bureau as a separate program.

President Nixon's appointee for Women's Bureau director, Democrat and former head of the National Education Association Elizabeth Duncan Koontz, used the Women's Bureau's fiftieth anniversary conference in 1970 to endorse publicly the Equal Rights Amendment. The EEOC's revised guidelines on sex discrimination in 1969 reversed previous rulings that protective labor legislation did not constitute discrimination. This policy reversal came in response to a trend in court cases finding protective labor laws invalid under Title VII of the 1964 Civil Rights Act.[1] Moreover, although a Democrat, Koontz functioned in the Republican administration that repudiated the interest group politics of the New Frontier and Great Society. The fiftieth anniversary conference's theme, "Womanpower—A National Resource," which summarized the postwar economic planning focus of the chief executive—addressing the educational and training needs of women—served as a forum for a dramatic reversal on the ERA.

Koontz urged Secretary of Labor George Schultz to get President Nixon's permission for such an announcement because of "the exceptional opportunity for the Administration to demonstrate its serious concern for questions many women's groups are posing."[2] In explaining the Women's Bureau's reversal on the ERA to the public, Koontz referred to the action of the courts and the EEOC.[3]

Once again, a Women's Bureau director held up women's organizations as a justification for a policy. This reliance on constituency groups did not change over time, although the particular groups did. The Labor Department's ERA reversal jeopardized alliances with traditional policy partners, the National Council of Catholic Women, the National Council of Negro Women, and the National Council of Jewish Women. These organizations maintained support for protective labor laws and opposed the activities at the 1970 conference that, according to Olya Margolin, ignored the hardships of low-income women.[4] Margolin felt the same way about the fortieth anniversary conference organized by the Women's Bureau's Republican director, Alice Leopold, in 1960. Let down again by Bureau policy shifts in another Republican administration, protective legislation proponents met at the 1970 conference to organize the Committee Against the Repeal of Protective Legislation. Despite the activities of traditional allies, the Women's Bureau continued to build networks with state commissions on the status of women and attendant permanent institutions, such as the Women's Division in the Human Rights Department in Minnesota and the Women's Division in the Bureau of Employment Services in Ohio. In its continuing role as a supporter of programs in the states, the Women's Bureau found new policy partners. Regional representatives built relationships with local NOW branches in the 1970s.

In spite of the networking with its new allies from the women's movement, the Women's Bureau could not regain an independent program during Koontz's tenure as director and more and more of its functions dissolved into the work of other agencies. Consequently, programs did not expand to accommodate the flurry of activism started by the women's movement; personnel remained at seventy-five to eighty people. Instead, over time the Women's Bureau became, to borrow Esther Peterson's phrase, the "staff arm" of the Labor

Department as an expert on women. By the mid-1970s, the director of the Women's Bureau, still a political appointee, served as deputy assistant secretary for labor standards and special counselor to the secretary for women's programs, indicating the integration of women's issues throughout the Labor Department.

However, in true bureaucratic fashion, the Women's Bureau expanded its technical expertise to include the ERA after Congress passed the amendment for ratification by the states in 1972. Traditional allies abandoned the cause to retain protective labor laws after the Supreme Court invalidated such laws as violations of Title VII in 1971 and by 1972 joined emerging women's rights networks in the states. Established networks with women's organizations, state labor departments, and women's divisions in state governments enabled the Women's Bureau to become part of emerging ERA coalitions. In 1975, the Women's Bureau listed a program goal "to expand technical assistance in areas which would be affected by the Equal Rights Amendment."[5] The persistent practice of "linking government and the grassroots" has kept the Women's Bureau open for business to celebrate another anniversary, its eightieth in 2000.

Notes

INTRODUCTION

1. Diana Jenkins, interview with the author, Columbus, Ohio, August 5, 1997.

2. Women's Bureau, U.S. Department of Labor, *Working Women Count! A Report to the Nation* (Washington, D.C.: GPO, 1994).

3. Ibid., 5.

4. Dorothy Sue Cobble, "Recapturing Working-Class Feminism: Union Women in the Postwar Era," in Joanne Meyerowitz, ed., *Not June Cleaver: Women and Gender in Postwar America, 1945-1960* (Philadelphia: Temple University Press, 1994), 57-83; Nancy Gabin, *Feminism in the Labor Movement: Women and the United Auto Workers, 1935-1975* (Ithaca, N.Y.: Cornell University Press, 1990); Susan Levine, *Degrees of Equality: The American Association of University Women and the Challenge of Twentieth Century Feminism* (Philadelphia: Temple University Press, 1995); Susan Lynn, *Progressive Women in Conservative Times: Racial Justice, Peace, and Feminism, 1945 to the 1960s* (New Brunswick, N.J.: Rutgers University Press, 1992); Leila J. Rupp and Verta Taylor, *Survival in the Doldrums: The American Women's Rights Movement, 1945 to the 1960s* (New York: Oxford University Press, 1987).

5. See Cynthia Harrison, *On Account of Sex: The Politics of Women's Issues, 1945-1968* (Berkeley: University of California Press, 1988); Patricia Zelman, *Women, Work, and National Policy: The Kennedy-Johnson Years* (Ann Arbor: UMI Research Press, 1982).

6. Historians accept Judith Sealander's analysis of the Women's Bureau's ineffectiveness during the postwar years; see *As Minority Becomes Majority: Federal Reaction to the Phenomenon of Women in the Work Force, 1920-1963* (Westport, Conn.: Greenwood Press, 1983).

7. Alice Kessler-Harris, *A Woman's Wage: Historical Meanings and Social Consequences* (Lexington: The University of Kentucky Press, 1990), 99-108.

8. Theda Skocpol explains the structured policy approach in *Protecting Soldiers and Mothers: The Political Origins of Social Policy in the United States* (Cambridge, Mass.: Harvard University Press, 1992).

9. Recent publications examining the development and implications of maternalist social policies include: Ellen Fitzpatrick, *Endless Crusade: Women Social Scientists and Progressive Reform* (New York: Oxford University Press, 1990); Skocpol, *Protecting Soldiers and Mothers;* Sonya Michel, "The Limits of Maternalism: Policies toward American Wage-Earning Mothers during the Progressive Era," in Seth Koven and Sonya Michel, eds., *Mothers of a New World: Maternalist Politics and the Origins*

of Welfare States (New York: Routledge, 1993), 277–320; Gwendolyn Mink, *The Wages of Motherhood: Inequality in the Welfare State, 1917–1942* (Ithaca, N.Y.: Cornell University Press, 1995); Alice Kessler-Harris, "The Paradox of Motherhood: Night Work Restrictions in the United States," in Ulla Wikander, Alice Kessler-Harris, and Jane Lewis, eds., *Protecting Women: Labor Legislation in Europe, the United States, and Australia, 1880-1920* (Urbana: University of Illinois Press, 1995), 337–57.

10. Women in Industry Service, *First Annual Report of the Director to the Secretary of Labor for the Fiscal Year Ended June 30, 1918* (Washington, D.C.: GPO, 1918), 3.

11. Robin Muncy, *Creating a Female Dominion in American Reform, 1890-1935* (New York: Oxford University Press, 1991).

12. For an overview of the difference versus equal rights debate after 1920, see Nancy Cott, *The Grounding of Modern Feminism* (New Haven, Conn.: Yale University Press, 1987).

13. Zelman, *Women, Work, and National Policy,* and Sealander, *Minority Becomes Majority,* recognize the Women's Bureau's efforts to address discriminatory public policies.

14. Mary Anderson, "The Effect of the So-Called Married Woman Bill on Business in General," speech, February 10, 1940, Women's Bureau Records, 1918-1965, University Publications of America, reel 16 (hereafter cited as WB-UPA).

15. Sealander, *Minority Becomes Majority,* 163.

16. Zelman, *Women, Work, and National Policy,* 12.

17. Mink, *The Wages of Motherhood,* viii–ix.

18. Georgia Duerst-Lahti, "The Government's Role in Building the Women's Movement," *Political Science Quarterly* 104, no. 2 (1989): 253.

19. Ibid. Ann Costain, *Inviting Women's Rebellion: A Political Process Interpretation of the Women's Movement* (Baltimore: Johns Hopkins University Press, 1992), also provides an analysis of government involvement in mobilizing grassroots feminism.

CHAPTER 1

1. *New York Times,* April 8, 1943, p. 1, 16.

2. Roberta Spalter-Roth and Ronnee Schreiber, "Outsider Issues and Insider Tactics: Strategic Tensions in the Women's Policy Network during the 1980s," in Myra Marx Ferree and Patricia Yancey Martin, eds., *Feminist Organizations: Harvest of the New Women's Movement* (Philadelphia: Temple University Press, 1995), 113–14.

3. Karen Anderson, *Wartime Women: Sex Roles, Family Relations, and the Status of Women during World War II* (Westport, Conn.: Greenwood Press, 1981), 178.

4. See Meyerowitz, ed., *Not June Cleaver,* for a revisionist history of the postwar period.

5. Susan Lynn, "Gender and Progressive Politics: A Bridge to Social Activism of the 1960s," in Meyerowitz, ed., *Not June Cleaver,* 103–27.

6. Early in the war employers preferred to hire men not eligible for military service. Industrial unions, too, aggressively sought to place prewar male workers in defense jobs; the United Autoworkers Union initially refused to support the recruitment of women for war work. For a discussion of employer and union resistance to female workers, see Ruth Milkman, *Gender at Work: The Dynamics of Job Segregation by Sex during World War II* (Urbana: University of Illinois Press, 1987), 67.

7. Government training programs initially accepted employer and union preferences and no centralized federal effort to mobilize women emerged outside of the War Manpower Commission and the Women's Bureau until 1943. See Anderson, *Wartime Women,* 30.

8. William H. Chafe, *The Paradox of Change: American Women in the Twentieth Century* (New York: Oxford University Press, 1991), 125.

9. Women's Bureau, U.S. Department of Labor, "Facts on Women Workers," September 30, 1946.

10. Frieda Miller, "Women in the Labor Force," *Annals of the American Academy of Political and Social Science* 251 (May 1947): 38.

11. Milkman, *Gender at Work,* 169.

12. D'Ann Campbell, *Women at War with America: Private Lives in a Patriotic Era* (Cambridge, Mass.: Harvard University Press, 1984), 11.

13. Anderson, *Wartime Women,* 55.

14. Women's Bureau, U.S. Department of Labor, *Preview as to the Transition from War to Peace,* Special Bulletin No. 18 (Washington, D.C.: GPO, 1944), 8.

15. Ruth Milkman, "American Women and Industrial Unionism during World War II," in Margaret Randolf Higonnet, et al., eds., *Behind the Lines: Gender and the Two World Wars* (New Haven, Conn.: Yale University Press, 1987), 168–81.

16. Bonnie Gutherie Smith to Lewis Schwellenbach, January 22, 1946, General Correspondence, Office of the Director, 1918–1948, box 12, file SM-SN, Records of the Women's Bureau, U.S. Department of Labor, Record Group 86, National Archives, Washington, D.C. (hereafter cited as General Correspondence, RG 86, NA).

17. Mrs. Benezue to President Truman, December 31, 1947, box 13, file BA-BC, General Correspondence, RG 86, NA.

18. Ruth Burns to Lewis Schwellenbach, August 11, 1945, box 12, file BS-Z, General Correspondence, RG 86, NA.

19. Suggested to the author by Renate Howe.

20. Women's Bureau, U.S. Department of Labor, "Biography of Frieda S. Miller," n.d., file Staff, Women's Bureau Office Files, Frances Perkins Building, Washington, D.C. (hereafter cited as WB Office Files).

21. Women's Bureau, U.S. Department of Labor, "Constance Williams," "Margaret Plunkett," "Mildred Barber," "Miriam Keeler," "Mary V. Robinson," n.d., file Staff, WB Office Files.

22. Women's Bureau, U.S. Department of Labor, *Women Workers in Ten War Production Areas and Their Postwar Plans,* Bulletin 209 (Washington, D.C.: GPO, 1946), 1.

23. *New York Times,* June 16, 1945, p. 16.

24. Mary V. Robinson to Helen Delich, January 6, 1947, box 36, file DA-DE, General Correspondence, RG 86, NA.

25. Judith Sealander, *Guide to Microfilm Women's Bureau Records* (Frederick, Md.: University Publications of America, 1986).

26. Mary V. Robinson to Natalie Kiliani, November 25, 1944, box 36, file KI-KL, General Correspondence, RG 86, NA.

27. Frieda Miller, "Unions Make Gains for Women Workers," prepared for the *Trade Union Courier,* WB-UPA, reel 19, 2-3.

28. Women's Bureau, U.S. Department of Labor, "Women Securing Equal Seniority Rights," press release, August 29, 1945, box 42, file Publications, General Correspondence, RG 86, NA.

29. Susan M. Hartmann, *The Homefront and Beyond: American Women in the 1940s* (Boston: Twayne, 1981), 54.

30. Anderson, *Wartime Women,* 31.

31. Campbell, *Women at War with America,* 142.

32. Ibid., 131.

33. Anderson, *Wartime Women,* 170.

34. Frieda Miller to Ewan Clague, June 25, 1945, Subject Files of the Director, 1919-1948, box 31, file Social Security Board, RG 86, NA (hereafter cited as Subject Files).

35. Frieda Miller to Boris Stern, May 7, 1946, box 27, file BLS 1948, Subject Files, RG 86, NA.

36. Caroline Manning, "Memorandum to the Regional Staff," January 25, 1945, box 42, file Regional 1945, Subject Files, RG 86, NA.

37. Frieda Miller to Elizabeth Brady, April 12, 1945, box 20, file BLS 1946, Subject Files, RG 86, NA.

38. Frieda Miller to Ewan Clague, November 27, 1946, box 20, file BLS 1946, Subject Files, RG 86, NA.

39. For a discussion of federal employment policy in the postwar years, see Gary Mucciaroni, *The Political Failure of Employment Policy, 1945–1982* (Pittsburgh: University of Pittsburgh Press, 1992); Otis L. Graham Jr., *Toward a Planned Society: From Roosevelt to Nixon* (1976; reprint, New York: Oxford University Press, 1979); and Margaret Weir, *Politics and Jobs: The Boundaries of Employment Policy in the United States* (Princeton, N.J.: Princeton University Press, 1992).

40. Constance Williams to Emile Benoit-Smullyan, October 8, 1945, box 20, file BLS 1945, Subject Files, RG 86, NA.

41. Frieda Miller to Ewan Clague, November 27, 1946.

42. Kathryn Blood, "Jobs—A Look into the Future," *Glamour* (January 1945), 3.

43. Ibid.

44. Ibid.

45. Women's Bureau, U.S. Department of Labor, *The Outlook for Women in the Medical Services: Physicians,* Bulletin 203-7 (Washington, D.C.: GPO, 1945), 18.

46. Women's Bureau, U.S. Department of Labor, *The Outlook for Women in Chemistry,* Bulletin 223-2 (Washington, D.C.: GPO, 1948).

47. Mrs. P. W. Sikes to Secretary of Labor (Maurice Tobin), November 17, 1947, box 14, General Correspondence, RG 86, NA.

48. Miller to Mrs. P. W. Sikes, November 26, 1947, box 14, General Correspondence, RG 86, NA.

49. Women's Bureau, U.S. Department of Labor, *Twenty-Ninth Annual Report for Fiscal Year Ended June 30, 1947* (Washington, D.C.: GPO, 1947), 7.

50. "Draft Equal Pay Bill," n.d., box 2, file Social Legislation Misc., 1943-46, Records of the National Council of Jewish Women—Washington Office, Library of Congress, Washington, D.C. (hereafter cited as NCJW Papers).

51. Frieda Miller, "Statement before the Subcommittee of the Senate Committee on Education and Labor in Support of S. 1178, the Women's Equal Pay Act of 1945," October 29, 1945, box 8, file 168, Frieda Miller Papers, Schlesinger Library, Cambridge, Mass. (hereafter cited as Frieda Miller Papers, SL).

52. Milkman, *Gender at Work,* 174.

53. Gladys Dickason, "Women in Labor Unions," *Annals of the American Academy of Political and Social Science* 251 (May 1947): 73.

54. Dorothy S. Brady, "Equal Pay for Women Workers," *Annals of the American Academy of Political and Social Science* 251 (May 1947): 54.

55. Levine, *Degrees of Equality,* 3.

56. Ibid.

57. Lynn, *Progressive Women in Conservative Times,* 112.

58. Judith Paterson, *To Be Somebody: A Biography of Marguerite Rawalt* (Austin, Tex.: Eakin Press, 1986), xvi–xviii.

59. Milkman, "American Women and Industrial Unionism," 172.

60. Gabin, *Feminism in the Labor Movement,* 86.

61. Dorothy Sue Cobble discusses the importance of equal pay legislation to labor union women in "Recapturing Working-Class Feminism."

62. Gabin, *Feminism in the Labor Movement,* 93.

63. Ibid.

64. Dickason, "Women in Labor Unions," 76.

65. Frieda Miller, "Memorandum Postwar Program," August 22, 1945, box 26, file Labor Department—Assistant Secretary, Subject Files, RG 86, NA.

66. "Suggested Changes for Federal Jury Bills," December 9, 1947, box 10, file Equal Rights, General Correspondence, RG 86, NA.

67. *New York Times,* May 1, 1955, p. 85.

68. Women's Bureau, U.S. Department of Labor, "Reconversion Blueprint for Women," press release, December 5, 1944, box 50, file Publications,

General Correspondence, RG 86, NA.

69. Women's Bureau, U.S. Department of Labor, "Reconversion Blueprint for Women," December 5, 1944, WB-UPA, reel 8.

70. Women's Bureau, U.S. Department of Labor, "Women Union Leaders Speak: Conference Proceedings," April 18–19, 1945, WB-UPA, reel 10.

71. Anne Larrabee to Rochelle Rodd Gachet, February 20, 1946, box 58, file BPW 1946, General Correspondence, RG 86, NA.

72. Helen Mills to Frieda Miller, May 12, 1945, box 57, file AAUW Michigan, General Correspondence, RG 86, NA.

73. Frieda Miller to Mrs. Jasspon, January 24, 1945, box 57, file AAUW Tennessee, General Correspondence, RG 86, NA.

74. Kathryn Blood, "Postwar Employment Women in Industry," January 13, 1945, WB-UPA, reel 19.

75. Frieda Miller to Edna F. Kelly, September 25, 1951, box 20, file Parent-Child Legislation, Subject Files, RG 86, NA.

76. Sara L. Buchanan to Margaret Plunkett, September 29, 1950, box 3, file Division Women's Labor Law, Subject Files, RG 86, NA.

77. "Minutes Meeting of the Trade Union Advisory Committee, June 4, 1946," box 39, file Women's Bureau 1947, Subject Files, RG 86, NA.

78. Constance Williams to Frieda Miller, November 15, 1946, file Night Work, WB Office Files.

79. "Statement on Night Work Standards, December, 1946," file Night Work, WB Office Files.

80. *New York Times,* February 6, 1950, p. 2.

81. Ibid.

82. "Minutes December 7, 1948, Trade Union Advisory Committee Meeting," box A-37, file 146, Frieda Miller Papers, SL.

83. Ibid.

84. Ibid., 3.

85. Susan M. Hartmann, *Truman and the 80th Congress* (Columbia: University of Missouri Press, 1971), 5.

86. Anne Larrabee to Frieda Miller, February 14, 1947, file Attacks on the Women's Bureau, WB Office Files.

87. Ibid.

88. Ibid.

89. Ibid.

90. Sylvia Beyer to Frieda Miller, February 18, 1947, file Attacks on the Women's Bureau, WB Office Files.

91. Olya Margolin to Helen Raebeck, February 20, 1947, box 13, file Labor Department 1945–49, NCJW Papers.

92. Anne Larrabee to Frieda Miller, February 18, 1947, file Attacks on the Women's Bureau, WB Office Files.

93. *Congressional Record—House,* February 26, 1947, 1503.

94. The Women's Joint Congressional Committee was formed in 1920 after the passage of the Nineteenth Amendment to further legislation affecting women. Members of the organization in the postwar years were

as follows: American Association of University Women, American Dietetic Association, American Federation of Teachers, American Home Economics Association, American Medical Women's Association, American Nurses' Association, American Physiotherapy Association, Association for Childhood Education, General Federation of Women's Clubs, Girls' Friendly Society of the U.S.A., National Association of Nursery Education, National Board of the Young Women's Christian Association, National Congress of Parents and Teachers, National Consumers' League, National Council of Jewish Women, National Education Association, National Federation of Business and Professional Women's Clubs, National League of Women Voters, National Service Star Legion, National Women's Trade Union League of America, United Council of Church Women, Women's National Homeopathic Fraternity.

95. Olya Margolin to Helen Raebeck, February 20, 1947, file Attacks on the Women's Bureau, WB Office Files.

96. Anne Larrabee to Frieda Miller, February 21, 1947, file Attacks on the Women's Bureau, WB Office Files.

97. "Minutes of the Women's Joint Congressional Committee, December 8, 1947," box 6, file WJCC Minutes 1947, NCJW Papers.

98. Ibid.

99. Women's Bureau, U.S. Department of Labor, *Equal Pay for Women in War Industries*, Bulletin 196 (Washington, D.C.: GPO, 1942), 17.

100. Women's Bureau, U.S. Department of Labor, "Frieda Miller," file Staff, WB Office Files.

101. Frieda Miller to Zebulon Weaver, March 20, 1945, box 19, file Equal Rights January–November 1945, General Correspondence, RG 86, NA.

102. Pauline Tompkins, "Frieda Miller," in Edward James and Janet James, eds., *Notable American Women, 1607–1950: A Biographical Dictionary* (Cambridge, Mass.: Harvard University Press, 1971).

103. U.S. Senate, *Hearing before a Subcommittee of the Committee on the Judiciary on S.J. Res. 61*, 79th Cong., 1st sess., September 28, 1945, 8.

104. Ibid., 4.

105. Miller to Zebulon Weaver, 2.

106. "Excerpt Letter from Secretary Perkins on Equal Opportunity May 1946," box 11, file Civil Service Commission, Office Files of the Director, RG 86, NA.

107. "Suggestions Made at Meeting of Temporary Steering Committee, September, 28, 1944," box 10, file ERA Correspondence, 1944-49, NCJW Papers.

108. Frieda Miller to Mr. Moran, August 17, 1945, file Attacks on the Women's Bureau, WB Office Files.

109. Ibid.

110. Women's Bureau, U.S. Department of Labor, "Q and A on H.R. 2007," press release, December 30, 1947, box 19, file Publications, General Correspondence, RG 86, NA.

111. Women's Bureau, U.S. Department of Labor, "A New Bill on the Status of Women," press release, March 18, 1947, box 19, file Publications, General Correspondence, RG 86, NA.

112. Dorothy McAllistor to Presidents and Representatives of Member Organizations of the National Committee to Defeat the Unequal Rights Amendment, January 18, 1947, box 16, file National Committee on the Status of Women, NCJW Papers.

113. Marjorie Temple to Sarah Hughes, August 23, 1951, box Sarah Hughes, file Legislation 1951–52, National Federation of Business and Professional Women's Clubs Papers, Washington, D.C. (hereafter cited as BPW Papers).

114. Sarah Hughes to Marjorie Temple, November 14, 1951, box Sarah Hughes, file Legislation 1951–52, BPW Papers.

115. *New York Times,* June 18, 1951, p. 8.

116. Legislative Steering Committee, "Legislative Steering Committee Minutes, January 1953," BPW Papers.

117. Legislative Steering Committee, "Legislative Steering Committee Minutes, January 1952," BPW Papers.

118. Sarah Hughes to Marguerite Rawalt, February 15, 1952, box Sarah Hughes, file Legislation 1951–52, BPW Papers.

119. Ronnie Steinberg, *Wages and Hours: Labor and Reform in Twentieth-Century America* (Westport, Conn.: Greenwood Press, 1982), 90.

120. U.S. House of Representatives, Committee on Education and Labor, 88th Cong., 1st sess., "Legislative History of the Equal Pay Act" (Washington, D.C.: GPO, 1963), 53.

121. "Excerpt Letter from Frances Perkins on Equal Opportunity, May 1946," file Women's Bureau History, WB Office Files.

122. Paul Burstein, *Discrimination, Jobs, and Politics: The Struggle for Equal Employment Opportunity since the New Deal* (Chicago: University of Chicago Press, 1985), 66.

CHAPTER 2

1. *Life* (August 5, 1957): 14.

2. Alice Kessler-Harris, *Out to Work: A History of Wage-Earning Women in the United States* (New York: Oxford University Press, 1982), 301.

3. Ibid., 303.

4. William L. O'Neill, *American High: The Years of Confidence, 1945–1960* (New York: Free Press, 1986), 43.

5. Rosalind Rosenberg, *Divided Lives: American Women in the Twentieth Century* (New York: Hill and Wang, 1992), 159.

6. Levine, *Degrees of Equality,* 98.

7. Rosenberg, *Divided Lives,* 151.

8. Kessler-Harris, *Out to Work,* 301.

9. Ibid., 303.

10. Robert Griffith, "Dwight D. Eisenhower and the Corporate Commonwealth," *American Historical Review* 27 (February 1982): 91.

11. Additional sources on policymaking in the Eisenhower administration include: Arthur Johnson, "American Business in the Postwar Era," in Robert Bremner and Gary Reichard, eds., *Reshaping America: Society and Institutions, 1945-1960* (Columbus: Ohio State University Press, 1982), 101-13; James L. Sundquist, *Politics and Policy: The Eisenhower, Kennedy, and Johnson Years* (Washington, D.C.: Brookings Institution, 1968); Graham, *Toward a Planned Society;* Chester J. Pach Jr. and Elmo Richardson, *The Presidency of Dwight D. Eisenhower,* rev. ed. (Lawrence: University of Kansas Press, 1991); Bradley H. Patterson Jr., "Eisenhower's Innovations in White House Staff Structure and Operations," in Shirley Anne Warshaw, ed., *Reexamining the Eisenhower Presidency* (Westport, Conn.: Greenwood Press, 1993), 149-67; Iwan W. Morgan, *Eisenhower Versus "The Spenders": The Eisenhower Administration, the Democrats, and the Budget, 1953-1960* (New York: St. Martin's Press, 1990); John W. Sloan, *Eisenhower and the Management of Prosperity* (Lawrence: University of Kansas Press, 1991); and Fred I. Greenstein, *The Hidden-Hand Presidency,* rev. ed. (Baltimore: Johns Hopkins University Press, 1992).

12. Jonathan Grossman, *The Department of Labor* (New York: Praeger, 1973), 69-71.

13. Ibid., 72.

14. Elsie George makes this argument about women in the Roosevelt administration in "The Women Appointees of the Roosevelt and Truman Administrations: A Study of Their Impact and Effectiveness" (Ph.D. diss., American University, 1972).

15. *New York Times,* October, 17, 1953, p. 32.

16. Women's Bureau, U.S. Department of Labor, "Alice Leopold," file Staff, WB Office Files.

17. *New York Times,* February 14, 1954, p. 1, 51.

18. Alice Leopold speech, October 1, 1956, box 21, file Speeches, General Correspondence, 1954-1956, RG 86, NA.

19. Alice Leopold speech, box 21, file Speeches, Office Files of the Director, RG 86, NA.

20. Alice Leopold, "Women in Management Jobs Today and What They Look Forward To," April 20, 1956, box 21, file Speeches, General Correspondence, 1954-1956, RG 86, NA.

21. Alice Leopold, March 21, 1956, box 21, file Speeches, General Correspondence, 1954-1956, RG 86, NA.

22. *New York Times,* July 31, 1956, p. 26.

23. U.S. Department of Labor, *The Anvil and the Plow: A History of the United States Department of Labor, 1913-1963* (Washington, D.C.: GPO, 1963), 165.

24. Ibid., 206.

25. Gary W. Reichard, *The Reaffirmation of Republicanism: Eisenhower and the 83rd Congress* (Knoxville: University of Tennessee Press, 1975), 233.

26. U.S. Department of Labor, *Forty-Second Annual Report for the Fiscal Year Ended June 30, 1954* (Washington, D.C.: GPO, 1954), 46.

27. Ibid., 35.

28. "Women's Bureau," reprint from *Tide,* October 17, 1947, box 46, file TI, General Correspondence, 1954–1956, RG 86, NA.

29. "Memorandum to Bertha Adkins Concerning the February 9th Conference," March 12, 1953, box 99, file Labor—Status of Women, NCJW Papers.

30. *New York Times,* January 22, 1954, p. 24.

31. Alice Morrison to Winifred Helmes, February 23, 1955, box 3, file 2-0-0-3, General Correspondence, 1954–1956, RG 86, NA.

32. "Excerpts from Daily Proceedings of the CIO Sixteenth Annual Constitutional Convention, 'Resolution No. 37 Women Workers,'" December 9, 1954, box 1, file 1-0-1-2-1, General Correspondence, 1954–1956, RG 86, NA.

33. Alice Morrison to Winifred Helmes, February 23, 1955.

34. Stuart Rothman to Leopold, January 28, 1954, box 3, file 2-A-7-2-2, General Correspondence, 1954–1956, RG 86, NA.

35. Alice Morrison to Alice Leopold, May 28, 1956, box 4, file 2-0-0-3, General Correspondence, 1954–1956, RG 86, NA.

36. Leopold to James P. Mitchell, February 18, 1955, box 4, file 2-0-0-3, General Correspondence, 1954–1956, RG 86, NA.

37. Levine, *Degrees of Equality,* 101.

38. Gabin, *Feminism in the Labor Movement,* 160.

39. Ibid.

40. Eugenia Kaledin, *Mothers and More: American Women in the 1950s* (Boston: Twayne, 1984), 38.

41. Rochelle Gatlin, *American Women Since 1945* (London: MacMillan Education, 1987), 7.

42. O'Neill, *American High,* 25.

43. Levine, *Degrees of Equality,* 85.

44. Ibid., 101.

45. Ibid., 45.

46. Lynn, *Progressive Women in Conservative Times,* 119.

47. Susan Ware, "American Women in the 1950s: Nonpartisan Politics and Women's Politicalization," in Louise A. Tilly and Patricia Gurin, eds., *Women, Politics, and Change* (New York: Russell Sage Foundation, 1992), 281–99.

48. Kaledin, *Mothers and More,* 33.

49. Caroline Davis to James P. Mitchell, June 30, 1954, box 60, file Women's Bureau, General Records of the U.S. Department of Labor, Office of the Secretary, RG 174, National Archives, Washington, D.C. (hereafter cited as RG 174, NA).

50. Selma Borchardt, vice president, American Federation of Teachers; Mildred Horton, executive secretary, Home Economics Association; Agnes Ohlson, president, American Nurses Association; Mossie Wyker, United Church Women; Elizabeth Magee, general secretary of the National Consumers' League for Fair Labor Standards; Margaret Mealy, executive secretary, National Council of Catholic Women; Katherine Engle, president, National Council of Jewish Women; Vivian Carton Mason, National Council of Negro Women to James P. Mitchell, June 30, 1954, box 86, file Correspondence 1954 to June 1959, NCJW Papers.

51. James P. Mitchell to Caroline Davis, June 30, 1954, box 60, file Women's Bureau, RG 174, NA.

52. James Mitchell to Rowland R. Hughes, May 10, 1954, file Attacks on the Women's Bureau, WB Office Files.

53. "Message from the President of the United States to the Congress of the United States, May 1954," file Attacks on the Women's Bureau, WB Office Files.

54. U.S. Department of Labor, *Forty-Fourth Annual Report for Fiscal Year Ended June 30, 1956* (Washington, D.C.: GPO, 1956), 155–56.

55. *New York Times,* September 30, 1954, p. 39.

56. "Biographical Sketch of Winifred Helmes," box 3, file 6-2-1-1, General Correspondence, RG 86, NA.

57. Winifred Helmes to Betsy Burke, February 19, 1954, AAUW Papers, reel 112.

58. M. S. Barber to Anna Behrens, July 17, 1956, box 1, file 1-0-1, General Correspondence, 1954–1956, RG 86, NA.

59. Jean A. Wells to Leopold, April 17, 1957, box 17, file Employment Characteristics, Subject Files, 1957, RG 86, NA.

60. "Women's Bureau," n.d., box 1, file 1-0-1, General Correspondence 1954–1956, RG 86, NA.

61. Leopold to Carol Cox, May 25, 1956, box 4, file 2-0-0-2, General Correspondence, 1954–1956, RG 86, NA.

62. Margaret Mealy to James P. Mitchell, September 19, 1956, box 3, file 2-A-7-2-2, General Correspondence, 1954–1956, RG 86, NA.

63. Alice Leopold, "Federal Equal Pay Legislation," *Labor Law Journal* 6 (January 1955): 8.

64. Laura Dale to Leopold, June 27, 1955, box 3, file 2-A-7-2-2, General Correspondence, 1954–1956, RG 86, NA.

65. Leopold to Stuart Rothman, February 8, 1954, box 3, file 2-A-7-2-2, General Correspondence, 1954–1956, RG 86, NA.

66. Leopold, "Federal Equal Pay Legislation," 31.

67. John Earner, "Equal Pay for Equal Work: Federal Legislative Activity, 1945 to 1962," December 14, 1962, Women's Bureau Reprint, file Equal Pay, WB Office Files.

68. National Committee for Equal Pay, "Minutes February 15, 1956," box 65, file Equal Pay, NCJW Papers.

69. Alice Morrison to Winifred Helmes, July 19, 1956, box 1, file 1-0-1,

General Correspondence, 1954–1956, RG 86, NA.

70. "Mrs. Bolton's New Bill," n.d., box 75, file National Committee for Equal Pay, NCJW Papers.

71. National Committee for Equal Pay, "Minutes January 28, 1955," box 75, file NCEP, NCJW Papers.

72. "Mrs. Bolton's New Bill."

73. Stella P. Manor to Walter C. Wallace, August 5, 1957, box 72, file Correspondence I–ME, Subject Files, 1957, RG 86, NA.

74. Alice Morrison to Leopold, December 10, 1957, box 74, file Correspondence T–Z, Subject Files, 1957, RG 86, NA.

75. "Brief Biography of Alice Morrison," n.d., box 3, file Legislation, General Correspondence, 1954–56, RG 86, NA.

76. Alice Morrison to Winifred Helmes, n.d., box 1, file 1-0-1, Subject Files, 1957, RG 86, NA.

77. Alice Morrison to Miriam Keeler, August 8, 1957, box 74, file Morrison 1957, Subject Files, 1957, RG 86, NA.

78. Alice Morrison to Frances Ambursen, October 16, 1957, box 74, file, Morrison 1957, Subject Files, 1957, RG 86, NA.

79. "Women's Advisory Committee," May 31, 1955, box 2, file Advisory Committees, General Correspondence, 1954–1956, RG 86, NA.

80. Leopold to Stuart Rothman, March 7, 1957, box 53, file Administration, Subject Files, 1957, RG 86, NA.

81. Winifred Helmes to Helen Loy, October 15, 1954, Alice Leopold Papers, box 1, file 8, Schlesinger Library.

82. Ibid., 48.

83. Women's Bureau, U.S. Department of Labor, *The Effective Use of Womanpower: Report of the Conference March 10 and 11, 1955,* Bulletin 257 (Washington, D.C.: GPO, 1955), 80.

84. Ibid., 5–19.

85. Ibid., 26–48.

86. Women's Bureau, U.S. Department of Labor, *Careers for Women in the Physical Sciences,* Bulletin 270 (Washington, D.C.: GPO, 1959), 1.

87. See U.S. Department of Labor, Women's Bureau, *Professional Engineering: Opportunities for Women,* Bulletin 254 (Washington, D.C.: GPO, 1954); *Employment Opportunities for Women in Professional Accounting,* Bulletin 258 (Washington, D.C.: GPO, 1955); *Employment Opportunities for Women Mathematicians and Statisticians,* Bulletin 262 (Washington, D.C.: GPO, 1957); *Careers for Women in the Physical Sciences.*

88. A. Sullivan to Leopold, n.d., box 74, file Correspondence T–Z, Subject Files, 1957, RG 86, NA.

89. "Women's Bureau Program Data, 1954–1959," n.d., box 1, file 1-0-1, General Correspondence, 1954–1956, RG 86, NA.

90. Neal A. Johnson to Leopold, September 12, 1957, box 74, file Correspondence, Subject Files, 1957, RG 86, NA.

91. Leopold to James E. Dodson, November 20, 1957, box 72, file Correspondence, Subject Files, 1957, RG 86, NA.

92. Alice Morrison to Leopold, July 9, 1957, box 53, file Administration, Subject Files, 1957, RG 86, NA.

93. Frances Whitelock to Leopold, June 7, 1957, box 53, file Administration, Subject Files, 1957, RG 86, NA.

94. "Members of the Field Staff," October 11, 1957, box 54, file Administration, Subject Files, 1957, RG 86, NA.

95. Winifred Helmes to Meribeth Cameron, December 7, 1953, AAUW Papers, reel 121.

96. Rocco S. Siciliano to Leopold, August 2, 1957, box 52, file Employment Opportunities, Subject Files, 1957, RG 86, NA.

97. Leopold to Seymour Wolfbein, January 8, 1957, box 52, file Employment Opportunities, Subject Files, 1957, RG 86, NA.

98. Leopold to Lila Durgan, December 19, 1957, box 70, file BPW, Subject Files, 1957, RG 86, NA.

99. Alice Leopold, "The Earnings Opportunities Forum for Mature Women," *National Business Woman* (July 1959): 7.

100. Women's Bureau, U.S. Department of Labor, "Organizations Sponsor Earning Opportunities Forum," press release, n.d., box 61, file Press/Radio 9, Subject Files, 1957, RG 86, NA.

101. Women's Bureau, U.S. Department of Labor, "What Your Community Can Do to Train Mature Women for Jobs," n.d., box 2, file Leaflets, Subject Files, 1957, RG 86, NA.

102. Marguerite Zapoleon to Leopold, December 3, 1957, box 52, file Employment Opportunities, Subject Files, 1957, RG 86, NA.

103. Leopold to Grace T. Elliott, September 9, 1957, box 70, file Correspondence A-Colleges, Subject Files, 1957, RG 86, NA.

104. Alice M. Anderson to Alice Leopold, November 26, 1957, box 74, file Correspondence T-Z, Subject Files, 1957, RG 86, NA.

105. Alice M. Anderson to Sylvia Pallow, December 6, 1957, box 62, file Speeches/Statements, Subject Files, 1957, RG 86, NA.

106. Alice M. Anderson to Leopold, September 6, 1957, box 61, file Radio/TV, Subject Files, 1957, RG 86, NA.

107. Alice M. Anderson to Leopold, June 27, 1957, box 61, file Radio/TV, Subject Files, 1957, RG 86, NA.

108. "Women's Bureau Program Data, 1954-1959," n.d., box 1, file 1-0-1, General Correspondence, 1954-1956, RG 86, NA.

109. Alice M. Anderson to Sylvia Pallow, December 6, 1957, box 62, file Public Relations/Speeches and Statements, Subject Files, 1957, RG 86, NA.

110. Anderson to Leopold, June 27, 1957.

111. National Manpower Council, *Womanpower* (New York: Columbia University Press, 1957). See also Susan Hartmann, "Women's Employment and the Domestic Ideal in the Early Cold War Years," in Meyerowitz, ed., *Not June Cleaver,* 84-102.

112. "National Manpower Council Information Memorandum No. 114," AAUW Papers, reel 145.

113. Ibid.

114. Olya Margolin to Helen Raebeck, June 9, 1960, box 98, file Labor—General, NCJW Papers.

115. Ware, "American Women in the 1950s," 291.

CHAPTER 3

1. Esther Peterson, 1981 speech, given to the author by Ruth Shinn.

2. Esther Peterson with Winifred Conkling, *Restless: The Memoirs of Labor and Consumer Activist Esther Peterson* (Washington, D.C.: Caring Publishing, 1995), 105.

3. Myra Marx Ferree and Beth B. Hess, *Controversy and Coalition: The New Feminist Movement across Three Decades of Change,* rev. ed. (Boston: Twayne, 1994), 59–61.

4. Peterson and Conkling, *Restless,* 95.

5. Alonzo L. Hamby, *Liberalism and Its Challengers: FDR to Reagan* (New York: Oxford University Press, 1985), 188.

6. Women's Bureau, U.S. Department of Labor, "Biography of Esther Peterson," file Staff, WB Office Files. For accounts of Esther Peterson's influence within the Kennedy administration, see Harrison, *On Account of Sex,* and Zelman, *Women, Work, and National Policy.*

7. Alan Shank, *Presidential Policy Leadership: Kennedy and Social Welfare* (Lanham, Md.: University Press of America, 1980), 237–41.

8. Ibid., 245. See also James N. Giglio, *The Presidency of John F. Kennedy* (Lawrence: University of Kansas Press, 1991), 97–121.

9. Transcript, Millard Cass Oral History Interview, July 14, 1970, by William W. Moss, Part I, p. 9, John F. Kennedy Library, Boston, Massachusetts (hereafter cited as JFK Library).

10. David T. Stanley, *Changing Administrations: The 1961 and 1964 Transitions in Six Departments* (Washington, D.C.: Brookings Institution, 1965), 3. See also Thomas R. Wolanin, *Presidential Advisory Commissions: Truman to Nixon* (Madison: University of Wisconsin Press, 1975).

11. Ibid.

12. Graham, *Toward a Planned Society,* 184.

13. Kessler-Harris, *Out to Work,* 312.

14. Jo Freeman, *The Politics of Women's Liberation* (New York: Longman, 1975), 29.

15. Paterson, *To Be Somebody,* 116.

16. Levine, *Degrees of Equality,* 146.

17. Gabin, *Feminism in the Labor Movement,* 220–21.

18. Faith Rogow, *Gone to Another Meeting: The National Council of Jewish Women, 1893–1993* (Tuscaloosa: University of Alabama Press, 1993), 185–87.

19. Paula Giddings, *When and Where I Enter: The Impact of Black Women on Race and Sex in America* (New York: William Morrow, 1984), 247–49.

20. Records of the National Young Women's Christian Association,

New York City, reel 298, Series III.C., Subject Files.

21. Lynn, *Progressive Women in Conservative Times,* 146.

22. Transcript, Esther Peterson Oral History Interview, February 11, 1970, by Ann M. Campbell, Part II, p. 36, JFK Library.

23. Peterson and Conkling, *Restless,* 96.

24. *New York Times,* January 28, 1961, p. 72.

25. Helen Kokes to Lawrence F. O'Brien, March 19, 1961, Central Subject Files, box 696, file Women, JFK Library.

26. Emma Guffy Miller to Bernice Pike, May 20, 1961, AAUW Papers, reel 106.

27. Emma Guffy Miller to Mrs. Forest, April 18, 1961, AAUW Papers, reel 106.

28. Levine, *Degrees of Equality,* 138.

29. Mrs. William Cooper, "Report on Conference at Women's Bureau, May 5, 1961," box 98, file Labor-General, NCJW Papers.

30. Kessler-Harris, *Out to Work,* 313.

31. Esther Peterson Papers, Schlesinger Library, Boston, Mass., box 2, folder 169 (hereafter cited as Peterson Papers, SL). Scholarship on the economic policies of the John F. Kennedy administration includes: Seymour Harris, *The Economics of the Kennedy Years: And a Look Ahead* (New York: Harper and Row, 1964); Ellis Hawley, "Challenges to the Mixed Economy: The State and Private Enterprise," in Robert H. Bremner, Gary W. Reichard, and Richard J. Hopkins, eds., *American Choices: Social Dilemmas and Public Policy Since 1960* (Columbus: Ohio State University Press, 1986), 159-82; Hobart Rowan, *The Free Enterprisers: Kennedy, Johnson, and the Business Establishment* (New York: G.P. Putnam and Sons, 1964); James Tobin, "The Political Economy of the 1960s," in David C. Warner, ed., *Toward New Human Rights: The Social Policies of the Kennedy and Johnson Administrations* (Austin: University of Texas Press, 1977), 33-41. See also Mucciaroni, *The Political Failure of Employment Policy.*

32. Peterson Papers, box 1, folder 23, SL.

33. Esther Peterson, "Looking Ahead to Tomorrow's Job Needs," speech, June 6, 1961, box 1, file 30, Peterson Papers, SL.

34. Transcript, Esther Peterson Oral History Interview, by Ann M. Campbell, February 11, 1970, Part II, p. 38, JFK Library.

35. Alice Morrison to Peterson, July 6, 1961, box 177, file Morrison, General Correspondence, RG 86, NA.

36. U.S. Department of Labor, *Forty-Ninth Annual Report for Fiscal Year Ended June 30, 1961* (Washington, D.C.: GPO, 1961), 6. Studies contrasting Eisenhower's economic policies with Kennedy's under the Employment Act of 1946 are Harris, *The Economics of the Kennedy Years;* Robert M. Collins, *The Business Response to Keynes, 1929-1964* (New York: Columbia University Press, 1981); Jim Heath, *John F. Kennedy and the Business Community* (Chicago: University of Chicago Press, 1969). See also Edward D. Berkowitz and Kim McQuaid, *Creating the Welfare State:*

The Political Economy of 20th Century Reform, rev. ed. (Lawrence: University of Kansas Press, 1992); Edward D. Berkowitz, *America's Welfare State from Roosevelt to Reagan* (Baltimore: Johns Hopkins University Press, 1991); and William Leuchtenburg, *In the Shadow of FDR: From Harry Truman to Ronald Reagan* (Ithaca, N.Y.: Cornell University Press, 1983).

37. Stella Manor to Frances Amberson, April 25, 1961, Office Files of the Director, box 154, file Administration 9-6, RG 86, NA.

38. Esther Peterson to James Dodson, December 15, 1961, box 157, file Administration 9-6, Subject Files, RG 86, NA; Women's Bureau, *Fifty-Fifth Annual Report for Fiscal Year Ended June 30, 1961* (Washington, D.C.: GPO, 1961), 293.

39. "Minutes of Staff Meeting, August 9, 1961," box 176, file Women's Bureau, Office Files of the Director, RG 86, NA.

40. Juliet Kidney to Esther Peterson, n.d., box 176, file Women's Bureau, General Correspondence, RG 86, NA.

41. Mildred Barber to Esther Peterson, December 6, 1961, box 169, file Women's Employment 5-6-5, General Correspondence, RG 86, NA.

42. Esther Peterson to Amelia Dearmore, November 14, 1961, box 169, file Women's Employment 5-6-5, General Correspondence, RG 86, NA.

43. Augusta Clawson to Peterson, October 30, 1961, box 169, file Women's Employment 5, General Correspondence, RG 86, NA.

44. Ibid., 2.

45. Augusta Clawson to Esther Peterson, October 30, 1961, box 169, file Women's Employment 5, General Correspondence, RG 86, NA.

46. Phillis Basile to Frances Ambursen, July 12, 1961, box 168, file Women's Employment 5, General Correspondence, RG 86, NA.

47. Phillis Basile to Esther Peterson, June 2, 1961, box 168, file Women's Employment 5, General Correspondence, RG 86, NA.

48. Phillis Basile to Frances Ambursen, July 12, 1961, box 168, file Women's Employment 5, General Correspondence, RG 86, NA.

49. Olya Margolin to Helen Raebeck, January 25, 1962, box 121, Helen Raebeck Correspondence, NCJW Papers.

50. Mildred Barber to Esther Peterson, March 14, 1961, box 154, file Administration-5, General Correspondence, RG 86, NA.

51. Olya Margolin to Helen Raebeck, July 7, 1961, box 98, file Labor—Women's Bureau, NCJW Papers.

52. Muriel Ferris to Lawrence F. O'Brien, July 15, 1961, box 374, file Equal Rights for Women, Central Subject Files, JFK Library.

53. Katherine Ellickson to Esther Peterson, March 31, 1961, box 157, file Administration 1-11-1, Office Files of the Director, RG 86, NA.

54. Gabin, *Feminism in the Labor Movement,* 188.

55. Transcript, Esther Peterson Oral History Interview, by Ann M. Campbell, February 11, 1970, Part II, p. 57, JFK Library.

56. Ibid.

57. David Lawrence to John F. Kennedy, March 1, 1962, box 206, file PCSW, Central Subject Files, JFK Library.

58. Frances Ambursen to Esther Peterson, September 6, 1961, box 6, file PCSW Memos, Peterson Papers, SL.

59. Brigid O'Farrell and Joyce L. Kornbluh, *Rocking the Boat: Union Women's Voices, 1915–1975* (New Brunswick, N.J.: Rutgers University Press, 1996), 127.

60. Pauli Murray, *Song in a Weary Throat: An American Pilgrimage* (New York: Harper and Row, 1987), 347.

61. "Background Information on the PCSW," n.d., box 1, file Background PCSW, Peterson Papers, SL.

62. Murray, *Song in a Weary Throat*, 352.

63. Paterson, *To Be Somebody*, 144. For a discussion of the National Woman's Party's response to the PCSW, see Rupp and Taylor, *Survival in the Doldrums*, 166–72.

64. O'Farrell and Kornbluh, *Rocking the Boat*, 177.

65. Harrison, *On Account of Sex*, 153.

66. "PCSW Background Paper, Document 4," August 24, 1961, box 9, file 7, Peterson Papers, SL.

67. June Sochen, *Movers and Shakers: American Women Thinkers and Activists* (New York: Quadrangle Books, 1973), 231.

68. Margaret Mead and Frances Balgley Kaplan, eds., *American Women: The Report of the President's Commission on the Status of Women and Other Publications of the Commission* (New York: Charles Scribner's Sons, 1965), 210.

69. Despite a penchant for advocating executive orders to institute swift action on women's issues, the PCSW declined to press for inclusion of "sex" in Executive Order 10925. Executive Order 10925 served as the model for the order creating the President's Commission on the Status of Women, but the subsequent deliberative body refused to ensure equal opportunity for women by adding "sex" to an order that prohibited discrimination based on race, color, national origin, or religion in employment under federal contracts, preferring instead to adopt another order encouraging federal contractors not to discriminate on account of sex. For a complete discussion of the commission's deliberations on this matter, see Harrison, *On Account of Sex*, 138–42.

70. O'Farrell and Kornbluh, *Rocking the Boat*, 127.

71. President's Commission on the Status of Women, "Summary Report and Recommendations, Committee on Protective Labor Legislation," March 26, 1963, box 3, file Meetings, PCSW Series, JFK Library.

72. Transcript, Esther Peterson Oral History Interview, by Ann M. Campbell, February 11, 1970, Part II, p. 43, JFK Library.

73. "Implementation of Commission Recommendations," n.d., box 10, Files of Deputy Director Mary Hilton, 1961–1967, RG 86, NA.

74. Mary Hilton, telephone interview, July 9, 1997.

75. Olya Margolin to Helen Raebeck, June 15, 1962, Helen Raebeck Correspondence, box 122, NCJW Papers.

76. Transcript, Esther Peterson Oral History Interview, by Ann M. Campbell, February 11, 1970, Part II, p. 53, JFK Library.

77. Olya Margolin to Helen Raebeck, August 6, 1962, Helen Raebeck Correspondence, box 122, NCJW Papers.

78. Esther Peterson to Leo R. Werts, July 5, 1963, file Equal Pay Activities, WB Office Files.

79. Laura Dale to Alice Morrison, September 29, 1961, file Equal Pay Activities, WB Office Files.

80. Harrison, *On Account of Sex,* 104.

81. "The Women's Bureau's Relation to the Equal Pay Act," June 20, 1963, file Equal Pay Activities, WB Office Files.

82. Esther Peterson to Ewan Clague, July 16, 1963, box 197, file Equal Pay, General Correspondence, RG 86, NA.

83. Esther Peterson to Clarence Lundquist, June 6, 1963, box 197, file Equal Pay, General Correspondence, RG 86, NA.

84. Mary Manning to Alice Morrison, August 9, 1963, box 197, file Equal Pay, General Correspondence, RG 86, NA.

85. Ibid.

86. Beatrice McConnell to Alice Morrison, n.d., file Equal Pay Activities, WB Office Files.

87. Philip Arnow to Tom Kouzes, August 6, 1963, file Equal Pay Activities, WB Office Files.

88. Beatrice McConnell to Alice Morrison, n.d., file Equal Pay Activities, WB Office Files.

89. Clarence Lundquist to Leo R. Werts, February 12, 1963, file Equal Pay Activities, WB Office Files.

90. Beatrice McConnell to Leo R. Werts, November 22, 1963, file Equal Pay Activities, WB Office Files.

91. Esther Peterson to Bess Dick, February 7, 1964, file Title VII Prior to 1967, WB Office Files.

92. Murray, *Song in a Weary Throat,* 356.

93. Ibid., 357.

94. Paterson, *To Be Somebody,* 154.

95. "U.S. Women Join Hands in Bi-Racial Civil Rights Drive," press release, United States Information Service, January 1964, Records of the National Women's Committee for Civil Rights, box 21, file U.S. Government, RG 86, NA.

96. "Role of the Women's Bureau in the Formation of the National Women's Committee for Civil Rights," July 26, 1963, Records of the National Women's Committee for Civil Rights, box 21, file Organizations, RG 86, NA.

97. Freeman, *The Politics of Women's Liberation,* 67. Gabin, *Feminism in the Labor Movement;* Costain, *Inviting Women's Rebellion;* and Susan Hartmann, *The Other Feminists: Activists in the Liberal Establishment* (New Haven, Conn.: Yale University Press, 1998) also credit status of women institutions for a revival of a gendered ideology.

CHAPTER 4

1. *Raleigh North Carolina News and Observer,* October 1, 1964, clipping, box 1, file 39, Mary Dublin Keyserling Papers, Schlesinger Library, Radcliffe College, Cambridge, Mass. (hereafter cited as Keyserling Papers, SL).

2. Freeman, *The Politics of Women's Liberation,* 49.

3. O'Farrell and Kornbluh, *Rocking the Boat,* 179.

4. For discussions of Johnson's War on Poverty, see Ira Katznelson, "Was the Great Society a Lost Opportunity?" in Steve Fraser and Gary Gerstle, eds., *The Rise and Fall of the New Deal Order, 1930-1980* (Princeton, N.J.: Princeton University Press, 1989), 185-211; Carl M. Brauer, "Kennedy, Johnson, and the War on Poverty," *Journal of American History* 69 (June 1982): 117-48; Mark I. Gelfand, "The War on Poverty," in Robert A. Divine, ed., *The Johnson Years: Foreign Policy, the Great Society and the White House,* vol. 1 (Lawrence: University of Kansas Press, 1987), 135-72; James L. Sundquist, *Politics and Policy.*

5. U.S. Congress, Senate, *Hearing before the Committee on Labor and Public Welfare,* H.R. 10809, 88th Cong., 2nd sess., April 3, 1964, 1.

6. Women's Bureau, U.S. Department of Labor, "Biography of Mary Dublin Keyserling," file Staff, WB Office Files.

7. U.S. Congress, Senate, Committee on Labor and Public Welfare, *Hearing before the Committee on Labor and Public Welfare,* H.R. 10809, 88th Cong., 2nd sess., April 3, 1964, 6.

8. Keyserling, "Economic Opportunity—A Challenge to Community," speech, November 24, 1964, box 5, file 127, Keyserling Papers, SL.

9. *Raleigh North Carolina News and Observer,* October 1, 1964, clipping, box 1, file 39, Keyserling Papers, SL.

10. Democratic National Committee, "Women of the USA: Partners in Peace, Achievement, and Opportunities," box 1, file 39, Keyserling Papers, SL. Susan Hartmann argues that Johnson took credit for advances in the status of women in "Women's Issues and the Johnson Administration," in Robert A. Divine, ed., *The Johnson Years: LBJ at Home and Abroad* (Lawrence: University of Kansas Press, 1994), 53-81.

11. Mary Dublin Keyserling, "Women's Stake in the Coming Election," January 1964, box 1, file 39, Keyserling Papers, SL.

12. Keyserling speech, May 25, 1964, box 5, file 127, Keyserling Papers, SL.

13. Mary Dublin Keyserling, "Economic Opportunity—A Challenge to Community," speech, November 24, 1964, box 5, file 127, Keyserling Papers, SL.

14. Women's Bureau, U.S. Department of Labor, *Future Jobs for High School Girls* (Washington, D.C.: GPO, 1966), 6-15.

15. Keyserling to John Leslie, October 20, 1965, box 43, file Meetings and Conferences, Subject Files, RG 86, NA.

16. Keyserling to Howard Rosen, October 26, 1964, box 9, file

Women's Employment, Files of Deputy Director Mary Hilton, 1961-1967, RG 86, NA.

17. Keyserling to Mark Battle, August 30, 1968, box 11, file Training and Promotion, Files of Deputy Director Mary Hilton, 1961-1967, RG 86, NA.

18. Hartmann, "Women's Issues and the Johnson Administration," 53.

19. Keyserling to John W. Reynolds, June 1, 1964, box 28, file Office of the Director, Subject Files, RG 86, NA.

20. Freeman, *The Origins of the Women's Movement,* 52.

21. Alice Morrison to Mrs. Gordon Prang, October 21, 1963, box 197, file Civil and Political Status, General Correspondence, RG 86, NA.

22. Women's Bureau, U.S. Department of Labor, press release, April 12, 1964, file Regional Directors, WB Office Files.

23. *Dallas Morning News,* January 19, 1965, clipping, box 1, file 39, Keyserling Papers, SL.

24. *Houston Chronicle,* clipping, February 18, 1965, box 1, file 39, Keyserling Papers, SL.

25. Keyserling to Elizabeth Carpenter, February 23, 1965, box 41, file Civil and Political Status, Subject Files, RG 86, NA.

26. Agnes Douty to Mary Dublin Keyserling, August 20, 1964, box 30, file Meetings and Conferences, General Correspondence, RG 86, NA.

27. Women's Bureau, U.S. Department of Labor, press release, May 18, 1965, file Regional Directors, WB Office Files.

28. *National Business Woman* (January 1964), 27-28.

29. *National Business Woman* (January 1963), 11.

30. Katherine Peden, telephone interview, August 12, 1997.

31. *National Business Woman* (March 1966), 1.

32. Wisconsin Governor's Commission on the Status of Women, "Interim Report, August 1966," box 55, Viola Hymes Papers, Minnesota Historical Society, St. Paul, Minnesota (hereafter cited as Viola Hymes Papers).

33. Florence Murray to Mary Dublin Keyserling, December 6, 1964, box 1, file 39, Keyserling Papers, SL.

34. Illinois Council on the Status of Women, Bulletin III, January 6, 1964, box 5, Viola Hymes Papers.

35. Karl Rolvaag, "Executive Order Creating a Commission on the Status of Women, November 12, 1963," box 52, Viola Hymes Papers.

36. Viola Hymes, "Report on the Minnesota Commission on the Status of Women," June 12, 1964, box 54, Viola Hymes Papers.

37. Minnesota Commission on the Status of Women, "Interim Report of the Minnesota Commission on the Status of Women, June 12, 1964," box 55, Viola Hymes Papers.

38. Minnesota Commission on the Status of Women, "Minutes of the Employment Committee," n.d., box 54, Viola Hymes Papers.

39. Jewelle Taylor Gibbs to Viola Hymes, January 26, 1964, box 54, Viola Hymes Papers.

40. Keyserling to Jo Ann Babbitt, October 25, 1964, box 54, Viola Hymes Papers.

41. Viola Hymes to the Babbitt School Board, November 9, 1964, box 54, Viola Hymes Papers.

42. Mary Lou Hill to Viola Hymes, n.d., box 54, Viola Hymes Papers.

43. Minnesota Commission on the Status of Women, "Minutes, Employment Committee of the Minnesota Commission on the Status of Women, October 23, 1964," box 54, Viola Hymes Papers.

44. Keyserling to Viola Hymes, December 1, 1964, box 28, file GCSW, Subject Files, RG 86, NA.

45. Viola Hymes to Keyserling, December 15, 1964, box 28, file Civil and Political Status, Subject Files, RG 86, NA.

46. Ellen Holstrup to James A. Rhodes, May 19, 1964, box 16, folder 11, MSS 353, Governor James A. Rhodes Papers, Ohio Historical Society, Columbus, Ohio (hereafter cited as MSS 353). Portions of the history of the Ohio Committee on the Status of Women described here appear in Kathleen A. Laughlin, "Sisterhood, Inc.: The Status of Women Commission Movement and Feminist Organizing in Ohio, 1964–1974," *Ohio History* (winter/spring 1999), and are reprinted with permission from *Ohio History*.

47. "Minutes, Luncheon Discussion on Ohio Commission on the Status of Women, Friday, October 8, 1965," box 1, file Minutes, 1965–69, MSS 426, Ohio Commission on the Status of Women Papers, Ohio Historical Society (hereafter cited as MSS 426).

48. Metropolitan Columbus League of Women Voters' *Monthly Bulletin* (November 1966), 2.

49. "Press Release March 24, 1966," box 1, file Historical Material, MSS 426.

50. Mary Miller to Mary C. Manning, April 11, 1966, box 1, file Historical Material, MSS 426.

51. Richard G. Zimmerman, "Rhodes's First Eight Years, 1963–1971," 58–73, in Alexander Lamis, ed., *Ohio Politics* (Kent, Ohio: Kent State University Press, 1994), 61.

52. "Minutes, Meeting to Discuss the Formation of an Ohio Citizen's Committee on the Status of Women," March 31, 1966, box 1, file Historical Material, MSS 426.

53. Ohio Governor's Committee on the Status of Women, "Interim Report of the Governor's Committee on the Status of Women," December 12, 1966, box 23, file 5, MSS 353.

54. "Plans for 1966–67 Legislative Year," box 7, MSS 403, Columbus branch of the National Council of Jewish Women Papers, Ohio Historical Society, Columbus, Ohio.

55. Ohio Women's Committee on the Status of Women, *Women in the Wonderful World of Ohio: Report of the Governor's Committee on the Status of Women*, box 23, file 5, MSS 353, 15.

56. Ibid., 46.

57. Ibid., 22.

58. Ibid., 18.

59. Ibid., 20.

60. Ibid., 19.

61. Zimmerman, "Rhodes's First Eight Years," 69.

62. *Women in the Wonderful World of Ohio,* 15–32.

63. Elsie Denison to Alice Morrison, November 23, 1965, box 43, file Meetings and Conferences, RG 86, NA.

64. Alice Morrison to Keyserling, January 18, 1966, box 52, file Conferences and Meetings, Subject Files, RG 86, NA.

65. Olive Furth to Keyserling, February 17, 1965, box 41, file Civil and Political Status, Subject Files, RG 86, NA.

66. *National Business Woman* (March 1966), 10–11.

67. North Carolina Commission on the Status of Women, "The Many Lives of North Carolina Women: Report of the North Carolina Commission on the Status of Women, 1964," box 54, Viola Hymes Papers, 15.

68. Dianne McKaig to Beatrice McConnell, December 1, 1964, box 29, file Legislation, Subject Files, RG 86, NA.

69. Agnes Douty to Regional Directors, July 6, 1964, box 28, file Civil and Political Status, Subject Files, RG 86, NA.

70. "Summary of Proceedings of the Conference of Governors' Commissions on the Status of Women," June 12, 1964, box 5, file 127, Keyserling Papers, SL.

71. *National Business Woman* (August 1964), 29.

72. *Milwaukee Journal,* September 22, 1964, p. 34.

73. O'Farrell and Kornbluh, *Rocking the Boat,* 178.

74. Keyserling to Willard Wirtz, May 3, 1965, file Title VII Prior to 1967, WB Office Files.

75. Willard Wirtz to Franklin Roosevelt Jr., August 9, 1965, file Title VII Prior to 1967, WB Office Files.

76. "EEOC Guidelines 1965," n.d., box 54, file Women's Issues, NCJW Papers.

77. Alice Morrison to Marguerite Gilmore, July 16, 1965, box 43, file Meetings and Conferences, Subject Files, RG 86, NA.

78. "Informal Remarks of Mary Dublin Keyserling at International Association of Government Labor Officials' Executive Board Meeting, December 6, 1966," file Title VII Prior to 1967, WB Office Files.

79. Women's Bureau, U.S. Department of Labor, "Suggested Guidelines for Investigation of Alleged Discrimination in Employment Under Title VII," file Title VII Prior to 1967, WB Office Files.

80. Keyserling to Richard Graham, September 2, 1965, box 51, file Women's Employment, Subject Files, RG 86, NA.

81. Citizens' Advisory Council on the Status of Women, U.S. Department of Labor, "Employment Opportunities for Women Under Title VII of the 1964 Civil Rights Act, October 1, 1965," file Title VII Prior to 1967, WB Office Files.

82. Keyserling to Willard Wirtz, May 3, 1965, file Title VII Prior to 1967, WB Office Files.

83. Citizens' Advisory Council on the Status of Women, "Employment Opportunities for Women."

84. Judith Hole and Ellen Levine, *Rebirth of Feminism* (New York: Quadrangle Books, 1971), 82.

85. Ibid., 86.

86. *New York Times,* September 3, 1965.

87. Olya Margolin to Helen Raebeck, n.d., box 155, file EEOC, NCJW Papers.

88. Olya Margolin to Keyserling, n.d., file Title VII Prior to 1967, WB Office Files.

89. *Congressional Record,* June 20, 1966, 1.

90. Catherine East, "Newer Commissions," 35–44, in Irene Tinker, ed., *Women in Washington: Advocates for Public Policy* (Beverly Hills, Calif.: Sage, 1983), 35.

91. Murray, *Song in a Weary Throat,* 362.

92. "Report of the Third Annual Conference on the Status of Women, June 28–30, 1966," box 54, file Women's Issues, NCJW Papers.

93. For an account of the formation of NOW during the Women's Bureau's Third Annual Conference for Status of Women Commissions, see John H. Florer, "NOW: The Formative Years: The National Effort to Acquire Federal Action on Equal Employment Rights for Women in the 1960s" (Ph.D. diss., Syracuse University, 1972), 39–42.

94. "Report of the Third Annual Conference on the Status of Women, June 28–30, 1966," box 54, file Women's Issues, NCJW Papers.

95. Betty Friedan, *It Changed My Life: Writings on the Women's Movement,* rev. ed. (Cambridge, Mass.: Harvard University Press, 1998), 104.

96. "National Organization for Women, June 29, 1966," file 893, Pauli Murray Papers, Schlesinger Library, Radcliffe College, Cambridge, Massachusetts (hereafter cited as Pauli Murray Papers, SL).

97. Kathryn Clarenbach to Pauli Murray, August 12, 1966, file 893, Pauli Murray Papers, SL.

98. Keyserling to Stanley Ruttenberg, January 24, 1966, box 54, file Employment-8, RG 86, NA.

99. Keyserling to Curtis C. Allen, August 26, 1966, box 57, file Public Information, Subject Files, RG 86, NA.

100. Keyserling to Joseph Goldberg, April 21, 1966, box 66, file Employment, Subject Files, RG 86, NA.

101. Jean A. Wells to Herbert Rosenberg, September 11, 1967, box 74, file Reports and Statistics, Subject Files, RG 86, NA.

102. Lee Rainwater and William L. Yancey, *The Moynihan Report and the Politics of Controversy* (Cambridge, Mass.: MIT Press, 1969), 184–86.

103. Esther Peterson to Edith Cook, April 8, 1964, box 37, file Training, RG 86, NA.

104. Esther Peterson to Stanley Ruttenberg, January 29, 1968, box 79, file Employment, Subject Files, RG 86, NA.

105. Keyserling to Stanley Ruttenberg, January 15, 1968, box 79, file Employment, Subject Files, RG 86, NA.

106. Isabel Striedel to Mary Dublin Keyserling, October 2, 1967, box 67, Subject Files, RG 86, NA.

107. Keyserling to Leo R. Werts, August 8, 1967; Mary Kay Ryan to Keyserling, August 8, 1967, box 66, file Administration, Subject Files, RG 86, NA.

108. Keyserling to Robert Goodwin, August 29, 1967, box 66, file Administration, Subject Files, RG 86, NA.

109. Keyserling to Curtis Allen, February 27, 1967, box 77, file Women's Status, Subject Files, RG 86, NA.

110. Esther Peterson to Stanley Ruttenberg, May 21, 1965, box 43, file Meetings and Conferences, Subject Files, RG 86, NA.

111. Friedan, *It Changed My Life,* 98.

112. Keyserling to Esther Peterson, August 6, 1964, box 28, file Employment Opportunities, Subject Files, RG 86, NA.

113. Willard Wirtz to Sargent Shriver, August 13, 1964, box 28, file Women's Employment, Subject Files, RG 86, NA.

114. Keyserling to Willard Wirtz, August 20, 1964, box 28, file Women's Employment, Subject Files, RG 86, NA.

115. Ibid.

116. Keyserling to Esther Peterson, March 30, 1967, box 69, file Cooperation and Liaison, Subject Files, RG 86, NA.

117. Beatrice McConnell to Leo R. Werts, August 12, 1964, box 28, file Employment Opportunity, Subject Files, RG 86, NA.

118. Keyserling to Albert D. Misler, October 23, 1964, box 28, file Employment Opportunities, RG 86, NA.

119. Keyserling to Willard Wirtz, August 20, 1964, box 28, file Employment Opportunities, Subject Files, RG 86, NA.

120. Keyserling to Willard Wirtz, August 5, 1964, box 38, file Women's Employment, Subject Files, RG 86, NA.

121. *Duluth News Tribune,* October 15, 1967, clipping, box 57, Viola Hymes Papers.

122. Esther Peterson to John Macy Jr., March 3, 1967, box 70, file Legislation, Subject Files, RG 86, NA.

123. *National Business Woman* (May 1964), 2.

124. *National Business Woman* (April 1964), 5.

125. Hartmann, "Women's Issues and the Johnson Administration," 53.

126. *BPW Action* (September 1966), 12.

127. Hole and Levine, *Rebirth of Feminism,* 86–87.

128. Friedan, *It Changed My Life,* 96.

129. Keyserling to Leo Werts, April 3, 1967, box 66, file Administrative Management, Subject Files, RG 86, NA.

Conclusion

1. Elizabeth Duncan Koontz to Eleanor Fowler, December 19, 1969, box 101, file Women's Status, July–December, Subject Files, RG 86, NA.

2. Elizabeth Duncan Koontz to Secretary George Schultz, June 4, 1970, box 112, file Women's Status, Subject Files, RG 86, NA.

3. Elizabeth Duncan Koontz to Patsy Mink, n.d., box 112, file Women's Status, Subject Files, RG 86, NA.

4. Olya Margolin to Bess Dick, July 27, 1970, box 54, file Women's Issues—General, NCJW Papers.

5. Women's Bureau, *Handbook on Women Workers* (Washington, D.C.: GPO, 1975), 394.

Bibliography

Interviews with Author

Hilton, Mary. By telephone. July 9, 1997.
Jenkins, Diana. Columbus, Ohio. August 5, 1997.
McClanahan, Mabel. By telephone. July 24, 1997.
Nadel, Ruth. By telephone. August 21, 1997.
Peden, Katherine. By telephone. August 12, 1997.
Peterson, Esther. Washington, D.C. April 9, 1989.
Shinn, Ruth. Washington, D.C. April 14, 1997.
Striedel, Isabel. By telephone. July 24, 1997.

Manuscript Collections

American Association of University Women. Microfilm edition. University Publications of America.
American Association of University Women, St. Paul Chapter. Minnesota Historical Society, St. Paul, Minn.
Columbus Section of the National Council of Jewish Women. Ohio Historical Society, Columbus, Ohio.
Hymes, Viola. Papers. Minnesota Historical Society, St. Paul, Minn.
Keyserling, Mary Dublin. Papers. Schlesinger Library, Cambridge, Mass.
Leopold, Alice K. Papers. Schlesinger Library, Cambridge, Mass.
Miller, Frieda S. Papers. Schlesinger Library, Cambridge, Mass.
Murray, Pauli. Papers. Schlesinger Library, Cambridge, Mass.
National Council of Jewish Women. Library of Congress, Washington, D.C.
National Council of Negro Women. National Archives for Black Women's History, Washington, D.C.
National Federation of Business and Professional Women's Clubs, Washington, D.C.
National Woman's Party. Microfilm edition. Microfilm Corporation of America, Sanford, North Carolina.
Ohio Bureau of Employment Services, Women's Division. Ohio Historical Society, Columbus, Ohio.
Ohio Commission on the Status of Women. Ohio Historical Society, Columbus, Ohio.
Ohio Federation of Business and Professional Women's Clubs. Ohio Historical Society, Columbus, Ohio.
Ohio League of Women Voters. Ohio Historical Society, Columbus, Ohio.
Peterson, Esther. Interviews, 1966-1970. John F. Kennedy Library, Oral History Program, Boston, Mass.

Peterson, Esther. Papers. Schlesinger Library, Cambridge, Mass.
President's Commission on the Status of Women. John F. Kennedy Library, Boston, Mass.
President's Commission on the Status of Women. Schlesinger Library, Cambridge, Mass.
President's Office Files. John F. Kennedy Library, Boston, Mass.
Rhodes, James A. Papers. Ohio Historical Society, Columbus, Ohio.
U.S. Department of Labor. Files. John F. Kennedy Library, Boston, Mass.
U.S. Department of Labor. Record Group 174. National Archives, Washington, D.C.
U.S. Department of Labor, Women's Bureau. Office Files. Washington, D.C.
———. Record Group 86. National Archives, Washington, D.C.
———. Records. 1919-1965. Microfilm edition. University Publications of America.
White House Central Files. John F. Kennedy Library, Boston, Mass.
White House Staff Files. John F. Kennedy Library, Boston, Mass.

GOVERNMENT DOCUMENTS

U.S. Congress. House. Committee on Education and Labor. "Legislative History of the Equal Pay Act." 88th Cong., 1st sess. Washington, D.C.: Government Printing Office, 1963.
U.S. Congress. House. "Debates on Establishing Women's Bureau in Department of Labor." 66th Cong., 2nd sess. *Congressional Record* (April 5, 1920), 59: 5873.
U.S. Congress. House. *Hearings Before the Subcommittee of the Committee on Appropriations on H.R. 3199 Department of Labor—Federal Security Agency Bill.* 79th Cong., 1st sess. May 22, 1945.
———. *Hearings Before the Subcommittee of the Committee on Appropriations on H.R. Departments of Labor and Health, Education and Welfare Appropriations for 1955.* 83rd Cong., 2nd sess. 1954.
———. *Hearings Before the Subcommittee of the Committee on Appropriations on H.R. 5046 Departments of Labor and Health, Education and Welfare Appropriations for 1956.* 84th Cong., 1st sess. 1955.
———. *Hearings Before the Subcommittee of the Committee on Appropriations on H.R. Departments of Labor and Health, Education and Welfare Appropriations for 1957.* 84th Cong., 2nd sess. 1956.
———. *Hearings Before the Subcommittee of the Committee on Appropriations on H.R. 7035 Departments of Labor and Health, Education and Welfare Appropriations for 1962.* 87th Cong., 1st sess. 1961.
———. *Hearings Before the Subcommittee of the Committee on Appropriations on H.R. 10809 Departments of Labor and Health, Education and Welfare Appropriations for 1966.* 88th Cong., 2nd sess. 1965.
———. *Hearings Before the Subcommittee of the Committee on Appropri-

ations, H.R. 7756 Departments of Labor and Health, Education and Welfare Appropriations for 1966. 89th Cong., 1st sess. 1965.

———. *Hearings Before the Special Subcommittee on Labor of the Committee on Education and Labor, House of Representatives, H.R. 3861, 4269 and Related Bills.* 88th Cong., 1st sess. 1963.

U.S. Congress. Senate. Committee on Appropriations. *Hearings Before the Subcommittee of the Committee on Appropriations Accompanying H.R. 3199 Department of Labor—Federal Security Agency Bill.* 79th Cong., 1st sess. June 14, 1945.

———. Committee on Appropriations. *Hearings Before the Subcommittee of the Committee on Appropriations, H.R. 10940.* 88th Cong., 1st sess. 1962.

———. Committee on the Judiciary. *Hearing Before a Subcommittee of the Committee on the Judiciary on S.J. Res. 61.* 79th Cong., 1st sess. September 28, 1945.

———. Committee on Labor and Public Welfare. *Hearings Before the Subcommittee on Labor of the Committee on Labor and Public Welfare, United States Senate, S. 882 and S. 910 to Amend the Equal Pay Act of 1963.* 88th Cong., 1st sess. 1963.

———. Committee on Labor and Public Welfare. *Hearing Before the Committee on Labor and Public Welfare. H.R. 10809.* 88th Cong., 2nd sess. April 3, 1964.

———. *Rept. 1464 to Accompany H.R. 14745.* 89th Cong., 2nd sess. April 28, 1966.

———. *Rept. 271 to Accompany H.R. 10496.* 90th Cong., 1st sess. May 22, 1967.

U.S. Department of Labor. *Thirty-sixth Annual Report for Fiscal Year Ended June 30, 1948.* Washington, D.C.: Government Printing Office, 1948.

———. *Forty-second Annual Report for Fiscal Year Ended June 30, 1954.* Washington, D.C.: Government Printing Office, 1954.

———. *Forty-fourth Annual Report for Fiscal Year Ended June 30, 1956.* Washington, D.C.: Government Printing Office, 1956.

———. *Forty-ninth Annual Report for Fiscal Year Ended June 30, 1961.* Washington, D.C.: Government Printing Office, 1961.

———. *Fiftieth Annual Report for Fiscal Year Ended June 30, 1962.* Washington, D.C.: Government Printing Office, 1962.

———. *Fifty-first Annual Report for Fiscal Year Ended June 30, 1963.* Washington, D.C.: Government Printing Office, 1963.

———. *Fifty-second Annual Report for Fiscal Year Ended June 30, 1964.* Washington, D.C.: Government Printing Office, 1964.

———. *Fifty-sixth Annual Report for Fiscal Year Ended June 30, 1968.* Washington, D.C.: Government Printing Office, 1968.

———. *The Anvil and the Plow: A History of the United States Department of Labor, 1913-1963.* Washington, D.C.: Government Printing Office, 1963.

U.S. Department of Labor. Women's Bureau. *Annual Reports, 1918–1932.* Washington, D.C.: Government Printing Office, 1932.

———. *Twenty-ninth Annual Report for Fiscal Year Ended June 30, 1947.* Washington, D.C.: Government Printing Office, 1947.

———. *Forty-seventh Annual Report for Fiscal Year Ended June 30, 1953.* Washington, D.C.: Government Printing Office, 1953.

———. *Fifty-fifth Annual Report for Fiscal Year Ended June 30, 1961.* Washington, D.C.: Government Printing Office, 1961.

———. *Preview as to the Transition from War to Peace.* Special Bulletin no. 18. Washington, D.C.: Government Printing Office, 1944.

———. *Changes in Women's Employment During the War.* Special Bulletin no. 20. Washington, D.C.: Government Printing Office, 1945.

———. *Employment Opportunities in Characteristic Industrial Occupations of Women.* Bulletin 201. Washington, D.C.: Government Printing Office, 1945.

———. *The Outlook for Women in the Medical Services: Occupational Therapists.* Bulletin 203-2. Washington, D.C.: Government Printing Office, 1945.

———. *The Outlook for Women in the Medical Services: Physicians.* Bulletin 203-7. Washington, D.C.: Government Printing Office, 1945.

———. *Women Workers in Ten War Production Areas and Their Postwar Plans.* Bulletin 209. Washington, D.C.: Government Printing Office, 1946.

———. *The Outlook for Women in Chemistry.* Bulletin 223-2. Washington, D.C.: Government Printing Office, 1948.

———. *The Outlook for Women in Architecture and Engineering.* Bulletin 223-5. Washington, D.C.: Government Printing Office, 1948.

———. *Professional Engineering: Opportunities for Women.* Bulletin 254. Washington, D.C.: Government Printing Office, 1954.

———. *Employment Opportunities for Women in Professional Accounting.* Bulletin 258. Washington, D.C.: Government Printing Office, 1955.

———. *Employment Opportunities for Women Mathematicians and Statisticians.* Bulletin 262. Washington, D.C.: Government Printing Office, 1957.

———. *Careers for Women in the Physical Sciences.* Bulletin 270. Washington, D.C.: Government Printing Office, 1959.

———. *Future Jobs for High School Girls.* Washington, D.C.: Government Printing Office, 1966.

———. *State Labor Laws in Transition: From Protection to Equal Status for Women.* Pamphlet 15. Washington, D.C.: Government Printing Office, 1976.

———. *Equal Pay for Women in War Industries.* Bulletin 196. Washington, D.C.: Government Printing Office, 1942.

———. *Report, Conference on the Effective Use of Womanpower, 10–11 March 1955.* Washington, D.C.: Government Printing Office, 1955.

———. *State Minimum Wage Laws.* Washington, D.C.: Government Printing Office, 1963.
Women in Industry Service. *First Annual Report of the Director to the Secretary of Labor for the Fiscal Year Ended June 30, 1918.* Washington, D.C.: Government Printing Office, 1918.
———. *Second Annual Report of the Director to the Secretary of Labor for the Fiscal Year Ended June 30, 1919.* Washington, D.C.: Government Printing Office, 1919.

BOOKS

Anderson, Karen. *Wartime Women: Sex Roles, Family Relations, and the Status of Women during World War II.* Westport, Conn.: Greenwood Press, 1981.
Berkowitz, Edward D. *America's Welfare State from Roosevelt to Reagan.* Baltimore: Johns Hopkins University Press, 1991.
Berkowitz, Edward D., and Kim McQuaid. *Creating the Welfare State: The Political Economy of 20th Century Reform.* Rev. ed. Lawrence: University of Kansas Press, 1992.
Burstein, Paul. *Discrimination, Jobs, and Politics: The Struggle for Equal Employment Opportunity since the New Deal.* Chicago: University of Chicago Press, 1985.
Campbell, D'Ann. *Women at War with America: Private Lives in a Patriotic Era.* Cambridge, Mass.: Harvard University Press, 1984.
Chafe, William H. *The Paradox of Change: American Women in the Twentieth Century.* New York: Oxford University Press, 1991.
Collins, Robert M. *The Business Response to Keynes, 1929-1964.* New York: Columbia University Press, 1981.
Costain, Ann. *Inviting Women's Rebellion: A Political Process Interpretation of the Women's Movement.* Baltimore: Johns Hopkins University Press, 1992.
Cott, Nancy. *The Grounding of Modern Feminism.* New Haven, Conn.: Yale University Press, 1987.
Dubofsky, Melvyn. *The State and Labor in Modern America.* Chapel Hill: University of North Carolina Press, 1994.
Ferree, Myra Marx, and Beth B. Hess. *Controversy and Coalition: The New Feminist Movement across Three Decades of Change.* Rev. ed. Boston: Twayne, 1994.
Fitzpatrick, Ellen. *Endless Crusade: Women Social Scientists and Progressive Reform.* New York: Oxford University Press, 1990.
Freeman, Jo. *The Politics of Women's Liberation.* New York: Longman, 1975.
Friedan, Betty. *It Changed My Life: Writings on the Women's Movement.* Rev. ed. Cambridge, Mass.: Harvard University Press, 1998.
Gabin, Nancy. *Feminism in the Labor Movement: Women and the United*

Auto Workers, 1935-1975. Ithaca, N.Y.: Cornell University Press, 1990.

Gatlin, Rochelle. *American Women Since 1945.* London: MacMillan Education, 1987.

Giddings, Paula. *When and Where I Enter: The Impact of Black Women on Race and Sex in America.* New York: William Morrow, 1984.

Giglio, James N. *The Presidency of John F. Kennedy.* Lawrence: University of Kansas Press, 1991.

Graham, Otis L., Jr. *Toward a Planned Society: From Roosevelt to Nixon.* 1976. Reprint, New York: Oxford University Press, 1979.

Greenstein, Fred I. *The Hidden-Hand Presidency.* Rev. ed. Baltimore: Johns Hopkins University Press, 1992.

Grossman, Jonathan. *The Department of Labor.* New York: Praeger, 1973.

Hamby, Alonzo L. *Liberalism and Its Challengers: FDR to Reagan.* New York: Oxford University Press, 1985.

Harris, Seymour. *The Economics of the Kennedy Years: And a Look Ahead.* New York: Harper and Row, 1964.

Harrison, Cynthia. *On Account of Sex: The Politics of Women's Issues, 1945-1968.* Berkeley: University of California Press, 1988.

Hartmann, Susan M. *Truman and the 80th Congress.* Columbia: University of Missouri Press, 1971.

———. *The Homefront and Beyond: American Women in the 1940s.* Boston: Twayne, 1981.

———. *The Other Feminists: Activists in the Liberal Establishment.* New Haven, Conn.: Yale University Press, 1998.

Heath, Jim. *John F. Kennedy and the Business Community.* Chicago: University of Chicago Press, 1969.

Hole, Judith, and Ellen Levine. *Rebirth of Feminism.* New York: Quadrangle Books, 1971.

James, Edward, and Janet James, eds. *Notable American Women, 1607-1950: A Biographical Dictionary.* Cambridge, Mass.: Harvard University Press, 1971.

Kaledin, Eugenia. *Mothers and More: American Women in the 1950s.* Boston: Twayne, 1984.

Kessler-Harris, Alice. *Out to Work: A History of Wage-Earning Women in the United States.* New York: Oxford University Press, 1982.

———. *A Woman's Wage: Historical Meanings and Social Consequences.* Lexington: University of Kentucky Press, 1990.

Leuchtenburg, William. *In the Shadow of FDR: From Harry Truman to Ronald Reagan.* Ithaca, N.Y.: Cornell University Press, 1983.

Levine, Susan. *Degrees of Equality: The American Association of University Women and the Challenge of Twentieth Century Feminism.* Philadelphia: Temple University Press, 1995.

Lowie, Theodore. *The End of Liberalism: Ideology, Policy, and the Crisis of Public Authority.* New York: W. W. Norton, 1969.

Lynn, Susan. *Progressive Women in Conservative Times: Racial Justice,*

Peace, and Feminism, 1945 to the 1960s. New Brunswick, N.J.: Rutgers University Press, 1992.

Mead, Margaret, and Frances Balgley Kaplan, eds. *American Women: The Report of the President's Commission on the Status of Women and Other Publications of the Commission.* New York: Charles Scribner's Sons, 1965.

Milkman, Ruth. *Gender at Work: The Dynamics of Job Segregation by Sex during World War II.* Urbana: University of Illinois Press, 1987.

Mink, Gwendolyn. *The Wages of Motherhood: Inequality in the Welfare State, 1917-1942.* Ithaca, N.Y.: Cornell University Press, 1995.

Miroff, Bruce. *Pragmatic Illusions: The Presidential Politics of John F. Kennedy.* New York: David McKay, 1976.

Morgan, Iwan W. *Eisenhower Versus "The Spenders": The Eisenhower Administration, the Democrats, and the Budget, 1953-1960.* New York: St. Martin's Press, 1990.

Mucciaroni, Gary. *The Political Failure of Employment Policy, 1945-1982.* Pittsburgh: University of Pittsburgh Press, 1992.

Muncy, Robin. *Creating a Female Dominion in American Reform, 1890-1935.* New York: Oxford University Press, 1991.

Murray, Pauli. *Song in a Weary Throat: An American Pilgrimage.* New York: Harper and Row, 1987.

National Manpower Council. *Womanpower.* New York: Columbia University Press, 1957.

O'Farrell, Brigid, and Joyce L. Kornbluh. *Rocking the Boat: Union Women's Voices, 1915-1975.* New Brunswick, N.J.: Rutgers University Press, 1996.

O'Neill, William L. *American High: The Years of Confidence, 1945-1960.* New York: Free Press, 1986.

Pach, Chester J., Jr., and Elmo Richardson. *The Presidency of Dwight D. Eisenhower.* Rev. ed. Lawrence: University of Kansas Press, 1991.

Paterson, Judith. *To Be Somebody: A Biography of Marguerite Rawalt.* Austin, Tex.: Eakin Press, 1986.

Peterson, Esther, with Winifred Conkling. *Restless: The Memoirs of Labor and Consumer Activist Esther Peterson.* Washington, D.C.: Caring Publishing, 1995.

Reichard, Gary W. *The Reaffirmation of Republicanism: Eisenhower and the 83rd Congress.* Knoxville: University of Tennessee Press, 1975.

Rogow, Faith. *Gone to Another Meeting: The National Council of Jewish Women, 1893-1963.* Tuscaloosa: University of Alabama Press, 1993.

Rosenberg, Rosalind. *Divided Lives: American Women in the Twentieth Century.* New York: Hill and Wang, 1992.

Rowan, Hobart. *The Free Enterprisers: Kennedy, Johnson, and the Business Establishment.* New York: G.P. Putnam and Sons, 1964.

Rupp, Leila J., and Verta Taylor. *Survival in the Doldrums: The American Women's Rights Movement, 1945 to the 1960s.* New York: Oxford University Press, 1987.

Ryan, Barbara. *Feminism and the Women's Movement: Dynamics of Change in Social Movement Ideology and Activism.* New York: Routledge, 1992.

Sealander, Judith. *As Minority Becomes Majority: Federal Reaction to the Phenomenon of Women in the Work Force, 1920-1963.* Westport, Conn.: Greenwood Press, 1983.

Seidman, Harold. *Politics, Position, and Power: The Dynamics of Federal Organization.* New York: Oxford University Press, 1970.

Shank, Alan. *Presidential Policy Leadership: Kennedy and Social Welfare.* Lanham, Md.: University Press of America, 1980.

Skocpol, Theda. *Protecting Soldiers and Mothers: The Political Origins of Social Policy in the United States.* Cambridge, Mass.: Harvard University Press, 1992.

Sloan, John W. *Eisenhower and the Management of Prosperity.* Lawrence: University of Kansas Press, 1991.

Sochen, June. *Movers and Shakers: American Women Thinkers and Activists.* New York: Quadrangle Books, 1973.

Stanley, David T. *Changing Administrations: The 1961 and 1964 Transitions in Six Departments.* Washington, D.C.: Brookings Institution, 1965.

Steinberg, Ronnie. *Wages and Hours: Labor and Reform in Twentieth-Century America.* Westport, Conn.: Greenwood Press, 1982.

Stewart, Debra W. *The Women's Movement in Community Politics in the U.S.: The Role of Local Commissions on the Status of Women.* New York: Pergaman Press, 1980.

Sundquist, James L. *Politics and Policy: The Eisenhower, Kennedy, and Johnson Years.* Washington, D.C.: Brookings Institution, 1968.

Weir, Margaret. *Politics and Jobs: The Boundaries of Employment Policy in the United States.* Princeton, N.J.: Princeton University Press, 1992.

Wolanin, Thomas R. *Presidential Advisory Commissions: Truman to Nixon.* Madison: University of Wisconsin Press, 1975.

Zelman, Patricia. *Women, Work, and National Policy: The Kennedy-Johnson Years.* Ann Arbor: UMI Research Press, 1982.

ARTICLES

Brady, Dorothy S. "Equal Pay for Women Workers." *Annals of the American Academy of Political and Social Science* 251 (May 1947): 53-60.

Brauer, Carl M. "Kennedy, Johnson, and the War on Poverty." *Journal of American History* 69 (June 1982): 117-48.

Cobble, Dorothy Sue. "Recapturing Working-Class Feminism: Union Women in the Postwar Era." In *Not June Cleaver: Women and Gender in Postwar America, 1945-1960,* ed. Joanne Meyerowitz. Philadelphia: Temple University Press, 1994.

Dickason, Gladys. "Women in Labor Unions." *Annals of the American Academy of Political and Social Science* 251 (May 1947): 70-78.

Duerst-Lahti, Georgia. "The Government's Role in Building the Women's Movement." *Political Science Quarterly* 104, no. 2 (1989): 249-68.

East, Catherine. "Newer Commissions." In *Women in Washington: Advocates for Public Policy,* ed. Irene Tinker. Beverly Hills, Calif.: Sage, 1983.

Freeman, Jo. "From Protection to Equal Opportunity: The Revolution in Women's Legal Status." In *Women, Politics, and Change,* ed. Louise A. Tilly and Patricia Gurin. New York: Russell Sage Foundation, 1992.

Gelfand, Mark I. "The War on Poverty." In *The Johnson Years: Foreign Policy, the Great Society and the White House.* Vol. 1, ed. Robert A. Divine. Lawrence: University of Kansas Press, 1987.

Griffith, Robert. "Dwight D. Eisenhower and the Corporate Commonwealth." *American Historical Review* 27 (February 1982): 91-130.

Hartmann, Susan. "Women's Employment and the Domestic Ideal in the Early Cold War Years." In *Not June Cleaver: Women and Gender in Postwar America, 1945-1960,* ed. Joanne Meyerowitz. Philadelphia: Temple University Press, 1994.

————. "Women's Issues and the Johnson Administration." In *The Johnson Years: LBJ at Home and Abroad,* ed. Robert A. Divine. Lawrence: University of Kansas Press, 1994.

Hawley, Ellis. "Challenges to the Mixed Economy: The State and Private Enterprise." In *American Choices: Social Dilemmas and Public Policy Since 1960,* ed. Robert H. Bremner, Gary W. Reichard, and Richard J. Hopkins. Columbus: Ohio State University Press, 1986.

Johnson, Arthur. "American Business in the Postwar Era." In *Reshaping America: Society and Institutions, 1945-1960,* ed. Robert Bremner and Gary Reichard. Columbus: Ohio State University Press, 1982.

Katznelson, Ira. "Was the Great Society a Lost Opportunity?" In *The Rise and Fall of the New Deal Order, 1930-1980,* ed. Steve Fraser and Gary Gerstle. Princeton, N.J.: Princeton University Press, 1989.

Kessler-Harris, Alice. "The Paradox of Motherhood: Night Work Restrictions in the United States." In *Protecting Women: Labor Legislation in Europe, the United States, and Australia, 1880-1920,* ed. Ulla Wikander, Alice Kessler-Harris, and Jane Lewis. Urbana: University of Illinois Press, 1995.

Laughlin, Kathleen. "Sisterhood, Inc.: The Status of Women Commission Movement and the Rise of Feminist Coalition Politics in Ohio, 1964-1974." *Ohio History* (Winter-Spring 1999).

Leopold, Alice. "Federal Equal Pay Legislation." *Labor Law Journal* 6 (January 1955): 8-31.

————. "The Earnings Opportunities Forum for Mature Women." *National Business Woman* (July 1959): 7-12.

Lynn, Susan. "Gender and Progressive Politics: A Bridge to Social Activism of the 1960s." In *Not June Cleaver: Women and Gender in Postwar America, 1945-1960,* ed. Joanne Meyerowitz. Philadelphia: Temple University Press, 1994.

Milkman, Ruth. "American Women and Industrial Unionism during World War II." In *Behind the Lines: Gender in the Two World Wars,* ed. Margaret Randolf Higonnet et al. New Haven, Conn.: Yale University Press, 1987.

Miller, Frieda. "Women in the Labor Force." *Annals of the American Academy of Political and Social Science* 251 (May 1947): 35–43.

Morgan, Iwan W. "Eisenhower and the Balanced Budget." In *Reexamining the Eisenhower Presidency,* ed. Shirley Anne Warshaw. Westport, Conn.: Greenwood Press, 1993.

Patterson, Bradley H., Jr. "Eisenhower's Innovations in White House Staff Structure and Operations." In *Reexamining the Eisenhower Presidency,* ed. Shirley Anne Warshaw. Westport, Conn.: Greenwood Press, 1993.

Robinson, Donald Allen. "Two Movements in Pursuit of Equal Employment Opportunity." *Signs: Journal of Women's Culture and Society* 4, no. 31 (1979): 413–33.

Rupp, Leila, and Verta Taylor. "The Women's Movement since 1960: Structure, Strategies, and New Directions." In *American Choices: Social Dilemmas and Public Policy since 1960,* ed. Robert H. Bremner, Gary W. Reichard, and Richard J. Hopkins. Columbus: Ohio State University Press, 1986.

Spalter-Roth, Roberta, and Ronnee Schreiber. "Outsider Issues and Insider Tactics: Strategic Tensions in the Women's Policy Network during the 1980s." In *Feminist Organizations: Harvest of the New Women's Movement,* ed. Myra Marx Ferree and Patricia Yancey Martin. Philadelphia: Temple University Press, 1995.

Tobin, James. "The Political Economy of the 1960s." In *Toward New Human Rights: The Social Policies of the Kennedy and Johnson Administrations,* ed. David C. Warner. Austin: University of Texas Press, 1977.

Ware, Susan. "American Women in the 1950s: Nonpartisan Politics and Women's Politicalization." In *Women, Politics, and Change,* ed. Louise A. Tilly and Patricia Gurin. New York: Russell Sage Foundation, 1992.

Weir, Margaret, "The Federal Government and Unemployment: The Frustration of Policy Innovation from the New Deal to the Great Society." In *The Politics of Social Policy in the United States,* ed. Margaret Weir, Ann Shola Orloff, and Theda Skocpol. Princeton, N.J.: Princeton University Press, 1988.

Zimmerman, Richard G. "Rhodes's First Eight Years, 1963–1971." In *Ohio Politics,* ed. Alexander Lamis. Kent, Ohio: Kent State University Press, 1994.

DISSERTATIONS

Florer, John H. "NOW: The Formative Years: The National Effort to

Acquire Federal Action on Equal Employment Rights for Women in the 1960s." Ph.D. diss., Syracuse University, 1972.

George, Elsie L. "The Women Appointees of the Roosevelt and Truman Administrations: A Study of Their Impact and Effectiveness." Ph.D. diss., American University, 1972.

Index